HOW
MANAGEMENT
WORKS

WITHDRAWN

HOW MANAGEMENT WORKS

THE CONCEPTS visually explained

Consultant editor Philippa Anderson

Senior Editors Chauney Dunford, Alison Sturgeon, Andrew Szudek
Senior Designer Mark Cavanagh
Editors Richard Gilbert, Katie John,
Victoria Pyke, Rachel Warren Chadd
US Editor Jennette ElNaggar
Editorial Assistant Maisie Peppitt
Designers Vanessa Hamilton, Mark Lloyd
Managing Editor Gareth Jones
Managing Art Editor Lee Griffiths
Jacket Designer Tanya Mehrotra, Surabhi Wadhwa Gandhi
Senior Jacket Designer Suhita Dharamjit
Managing Jacket Editor Saloni Singh
Senior DTP Designer Harish Aggarwal
Jackets Editorial Coordinator Priyanka Sharma
Publisher Liz Wheeler
Publishing Director Jonathan Metcalf
Art Director Karen Self
Jacket Editor Emma Dawson
Jacket Design Development Manager Sophia MTT
Producer, Pre-Production Andy Hilliard
Producer Rachel Ng

First American Edition, 2020
Published in the United States by DK Publishing
1450 Broadway, Suite 801, New York, NY 10018

Copyright © 2020 Dorling Kindersley Limited
DK, a Division of Penguin Random House LLC
20 21 22 23 24 10 9 8 7 6 5 4 3 2 1
001–316270–July/2020

A catalog record for this book
is available from the Library of Congress.
ISBN 978-1-4654-9231-9

Printed and bound in China

For the curious

www.dk.com

CONTENTS

MANAGING PEOPLE

COMMUNICATION

SELF-MANAGEMENT

Philippa Anderson (consultant editor) has a business degree and is a business writer and communications consultant, who has advised multinationals, including 3M, Anglo American, and Coca-Cola. She collaborated with Lord Browne, former CEO of BP, on his memoir, *Beyond Business*, and was a contributor to DK's *The Business Book* and *How Business Works*.

Alexander Black graduated with a degree in business communications, before moving to Tokyo to write for financial newspaper group Nikkei, Inc., and investment bank J. P. Morgan. She later worked for a global direct marketing specialist in the Asia-Pacific and is now based in London, where she writes on business and cultural history.

Pippa Bourne is director of Bourne Performance, helping organizations and individuals to succeed. She is also a Visiting Fellow at Cranfield University, where she supports the work of the Centre for Business Performance. Pippa has an MBA and a certificate in coaching and has many years of experience as a practicing manager.

Richard Ridout is a workplace technology and management transformation specialist. He has worked at senior management level across private and public industry sectors, encompassing scientific research, commercial property, entertainment, central government, education, and defense.

INTRODUCTION

Management is an instinctive human trait. Children at play will organize themselves to assume different roles, with one often taking the lead. As a business discipline, management came to the fore with the Industrial Revolution, when factory owners needed to maximize human resources. However, while it remains vital to business today, the role of the manager is changing. Managers still have to get the best out of people, but they do so by engaging and empowering the workforce rather than simply giving instructions. As a result, managers require a broad range of personal skills as well as technical abilities; they need to be sympathetic when appraising staff but ruthless when writing budgets—and be as mindful of company values as they are of profit.

For these reasons, being a manager requires patience, adaptability, and skill. It demands vigilance—the ability to keep track of a project while simultaneously monitoring the external operating environment, where changes in demand and competition can mean the difference between success or failure. There are various approaches that a manager can use to plan the future—from strategic management (see pp.30–31) to design thinking (see pp.112–113)—but none of these is a substitute for watching the market, understanding consumer needs, and being ready to adapt when necessary.

This book explains the changing world of management in a simple and graphic way. It covers the origins of management theory and explores the range of management roles, using examples from a variety of commercial, nonprofit, and government organizations. It aims to help students and aspiring individuals to understand what management is, and how it works. It also aims to help managers – both to navigate the business world and to improve their management styles. Chapter 1 explains management theory, while Chapter 2 shows how it can be applied in practical contexts. Chapter 3 examines people management; Chapter 4 covers communication; and Chapter 5 looks at personal responsibility.

MANAGEMENT BASICS

The Evolution of Management

The role of management first emerged with the advent of mass production and continues to evolve today, keeping pace with changing technology, employee expectations, demographics, and global politics.

Developing ideas

In the 18th century, economist Adam Smith recognized the need for workforces to be organized by task in order to maximize efficiency, which he described as the division of labor. As industries became more complex during the 19th century, attention turned to improving efficiency by minimizing labor use and standardizing and streamlining processes.

The mid-20th century saw the incorporation of many new fields of study into management theory. Psychology was applied to how people work; statistics to how processes were performed; and

A management timeline

As businesses have become more complex in order to compete and survive, the way they have been managed has constantly evolved. While the earliest theories concentrated on improving productivity through labor, later models looked at broader factors that help determine success. During this period, the role of employees has become more central, and there are now new views on the nature of competition itself.

MANAGEMENT ERAS

Execution era: pre-1900s–1960s
The period focusing on mass production, dominated by improving efficiency and ensuring consistency of production and predictability.

Expertise era: 1916–2000s
The rise of management theory, characterized by applying ideas from fields such as psychology and science to manage highly complex businesses.

Empathy era: 1990s–present day
An era emphasizing employee engagement and the value that staff bring as well as the worth of customer relationships in a transparent world.

Frederick Taylor's Scientific Management theory (see pp.24–25) views workers as machines.

1880

Henri Fayol's management principles (see pp.26–27) view employees as people who need managing.

1916

1913

The Ford assembly line marks the birth of mass manufacturing and the need to manage productivity.

1943

Abraham Maslow's hierarchy of needs (see pp.142–143) explores what motivates employees to perform better in their work.

ergonomics to make workplaces and machinery safer to use and more efficient.

Management theory also became more global at this time. As Japan rebuilt its industries after World War II, it rose to the forefront of new management thinking. Its larger firms ensured employees were engaged, empowered, and highly productive. Ideas such as lean production (see p.120–121) were widely adopted; likewise, zero waste and worker involvement.

Engaging employees

The 21st century is an era of accelerated change, with new technologies constantly emerging and disrupting existing markets. Management is less about lines of command and authority, and more about engaging people, building teams, and creating networks. This presents both opportunities and risks to managers, who must keep pace with the rate of change in order to lead their teams effectively.

> "**Management is the art of getting things done through people.**"
>
> Attributed to Mary Parker Follett, US management consultant

Japanese manufacturers develop management models to drive quality (see pp.40–41) and reduce waste and costs (see pp.120–121).

1950

Bruce Tuckman's FSNP model (see pp.146–147) explores the dynamics of team formation and management.

1965

The 7-S change model is developed as a tool to help managers coordinate and oversee change within their organization (see pp.96–97).

1980s

John Kotter's change model (see pp.94–95) reveals the importance of involving staff in organizational change.

1996

EXECUTION ERA PRE-1900s–1960s

EXPERTISE ERA 1916–2000s

EMPATHY ERA 1990s–PRESENT DAY

1960s

Douglas McGregor's X and Y factors (see pp.142–143) describe the role of encouragement and discipline in motivating employees.

1979

Michael Porter studies the competitive forces that influence how well an organization serves its market (see pp.80–81).

1990

Peter Senge's learning organization model (see pp.78–79) explains how learning helps organizations adapt to change.

2004

Blue Ocean Strategy, written by W. Chan Kim and Renée Mauborgne, (see pp.80–81) explains the need to find new markets rather than compete.

Management Roles

Since the late 20th century, the roles and boundaries that defined management have become blurred, yet the manager's fundamental function—to make things happen through people—is as vital as ever.

Management in flux

Technological and societal changes have meant that the authoritarian management roles of the past are now largely obsolete. In many organizations, hierarchies have been replaced by flatter structures, cross-functional teams, and informal networks. The rise of the "gig" economy means that a manager's team might include a mixture of employees, temporary staff, and contractors. Teams might be diverse, multigenerational, and even virtual. Nor is the workplace confined to an office; it could be in the home, a local café, or a train. The working day is not ruled by the clock—people can be "at work" 24/7—and technological advances mean that geography is no longer a limitation.

Control or empowerment

How managers work has also changed. Management is no longer top-down—rather, personnel are

Fayol's 5 functions

General and Industrial Management by French mining engineer Henri Fayol is considered to be one of the first key works on management theory. Published in 1916 and popularized in the 1940s, it outlined Fayol's five functions of management, which are still relevant today—albeit with an evolving interpretation for managers (see right). Another influential area of Fayol's work is his management principles (see pp.26–27).

17.6%
of the US workforce are managers and administrators

1. PLANNING

Setting objectives and methods was once the sole preserve of the manager, but teams are now fully involved in planning and setting goals and a course of action.

2. ORGANIZING

In the past, managers assigned tasks and duties, and workers had little say. Nowadays, managers empower their teams, and organization is a collaborative effort.

3. COMMANDING

Managers have left behind the top-down model of instructing and delegating in favor of aligning people, influencing them, and actively earning the leadership role.

4. COORDINATING

Previously, the manager ensured their staff worked to common goals. Today, a manager is more likely to create a vision, enthuse their staff, and lead by example.

5. CONTROLLING

Managers used to control their teams by setting targets measuring performance, but now managers prefer to use continual feedback, coaching, and recognition.

involved in planning from the outset to generate ideas, create buy-in, and build teams. Managers can no longer rely on authority, command, and control but must empower those under their care in order to create and maintain team cohesion and momentum.

In this new and fast-changing world, traditionally managed companies can be left behind; their inflexible structure may stifle innovation and prevent them from responding quickly or steering a different course when required.

> "What you do has far greater impact than what you say."
>
> Stephen Covey, US leadership expert, 2008

DIVERSIFYING ROLES

New technologies and trends in organizational culture mean that new roles are emerging while some traditional ones are disappearing. For instance, in addition to being central to the business world, managers are now vital in the nonprofit—or "third"—sector. A host of management roles exist in the public, private, and third sectors, such as account managers, diversity managers, and insight managers.

Leaders and Managers

Traditionally, leaders decided an organization's goals, while managers ensured that those goals were met. However, as working practices change, modern managers increasingly need leadership skills in their portfolio.

Combining roles

Until recent years, the distinction between the leader and a manager within an organization reflected traditional business structures. Today, as organizations have had to adapt to modern technology, forms of communication, and working practices, so the roles of leader and manager have evolved. Employees are now regarded as a collective source of creative energy within an organization and central to its success. In order to maximize the combined strength of their team and deliver performance, managers now often have to act as leaders.

As a result of the constantly changing way in which modern organizations need to be run, academics and consultants have studied the difference between leaders and managers. Many have concluded that the leadership/ management balance varies according to an organization's size, complexity, and industry. To be an effective manager today, however, a willingness to adopt leadership skills is essential.

Different purposes

Organizations need to draw on both leadership and management skills in order to accomplish their goals. Leadership offers the vision that sets an organization's course for the future. Leaders also provide effective responses to opportunities, crises, and change. In contrast, management involves day-to-day administration to achieve specific tasks to a particular standard—for example, setting budgets, planning workflows, or taking care of staff.

"**Leadership is the art of getting someone else to do something you want done because he wants to do it.**"

Dwight D. Eisenhower, US President, 1954

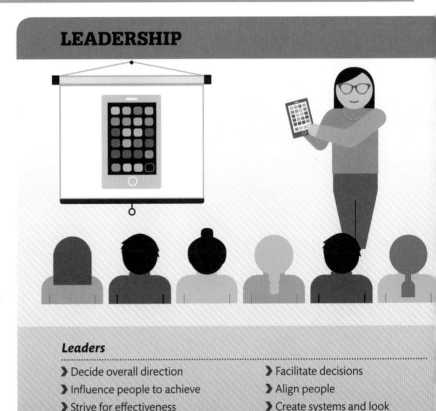

LEADERSHIP

Leaders

> Decide overall direction
> Influence people to achieve
> Strive for effectiveness
> Encourage change

> Facilitate decisions
> Align people
> Create systems and look for opportunities to improve

Leadership, management, and change

Leading management consultant John Kotter describes management as the process that keeps organizations running, whereas leadership is the task of inspiring and motivating employees. Managers help an organization cope with complexity, while leaders enable it to respond to change. As organizations evolve over time, so does their need for management and leadership (see right). Kotter illustrates this with a military analogy. During peacetime, an army can survive with good management at all levels and effective leadership at the top. However, in wartime, an army needs competent leadership at every level.

	LEVEL OF COMPLEXITY	
RATE OF CHANGE HIGH	**HIGH CHANGE, LOW COMPLEXITY** Strong, inspirational leadership necessary but little management	**HIGH CHANGE AND COMPLEXITY** Considerable leadership and management skills essential
LOW	**LOW CHANGE AND COMPLEXITY** Limited leadership and management skills required	**LOW CHANGE, HIGH COMPLEXITY** Considerable management required but little leadership
	LOW LEVEL OF COMPLEXITY HIGH	

MANAGEMENT

Managers

❯ Plan in detail
❯ Encourage people to perform
❯ Aim for efficiency
❯ React to change

❯ Make decisions
❯ Organize people
❯ Ensure that resources are appropriate and available

✓ NEED TO KNOW

❯ **Effective leaders** are prepared to allow their people to fail—as learning from failure leads to success. As Amazon CEO Jeff Bezos famously said in a letter to shareholders: "If the size of your failures isn't growing, you're not going to be inventing at a size that can actually move the needle."

❯ **Good management**, according to entrepreneur Paul Hawken, is "the art of making problems so interesting and their solutions so constructive that everyone wants to... deal with them."

Management Styles

The way in which managers lead a team is influenced by the needs and capabilities of the members and also by the circumstances. However, research has shown that there are times when a manager should adopt a specific management style to get the best from their team.

Varied approaches

All managers develop their own style of managing people and situations, which will vary depending on who those people are and what the situation demands. These approaches may also be influenced by prevailing management trends or changes to working practices (see box below). However, there may be situations when a manager's existing style is not the most effective, so they should be willing to change tactic.

In 2000, US consulting firm Hay McBer drew on a random sample of nearly 4,000 managers worldwide and identified six key management styles (see right). Daniel Goleman, author of *Emotional Intelligence*, described the findings in his influential article "Leadership that gets results" in Harvard Business Review. Their research showed that no single style was inherently right or wrong; instead, the most successful managers were those adept at shifting to the appropriate style for the particular situation.

"People come first."

Affiliative
The affiliative style is best used to motivate staff under stress and to bring an end to conflict. The manager should encourage the team to bond and hold informal meetings where members can share their views.

CHANGING APPROACHES TO MANAGEMENT

Until the 1980s, most managers typically remained behind their desks in private offices, at arm's reach from those they managed. Then, following an initiative at US firm Hewlett-Packard, managers were increasingly encouraged to leave their offices and to communicate with employees face-to-face, which became known as "management by walking around" (MBWA). More recently, however, email has made communication impersonal again, and so MBWA is back in fashion. In essence, it recognizes the importance of informal behavior in building relationships. For example, a manager may choose to wander to another floor and sit at a team member's desk for an informal meeting rather than call them to their own desk.

"Do what I tell you."

Commanding
This style is most appropriate in times of crisis or urgent change. The manager demands obedience, gives clear direction, takes tough decisions, and disciplines team members who underperform.

"Management is, above all, a practice where art, science, and craft meet."

Henry Mintzberg, Professor of Management Studies, McGill University, Quebec (2013)

Visionary

This style is an effective one for setting a clear direction or new standards of work. The manager should set out a clear, compelling vision and give the team freedom to work in their own way, experiment, and innovate.

Coaching

This approach is ideal when managing people eager to learn. The manager should focus on developing team members' skills and confidence, delegate interesting tasks, and forgive mistakes made during learning.

Democratic

A democratic style is best suited to stable working environments with experienced employees. The manager should seek team members' thoughts and ideas as part of building a consensus for action.

Pace-setting

The pace-setting style is ideal when team members are highly competent and motivated. The manager should set high standards from the start and maintain high energy, engagement, and motivation.

Situational Leadership

One of the best-known management models is Situational Leadership, by which managers adapt their leadership style according to the levels of ability and commitment among team members.

The adaptable manager

The Situational Leadership model was originally developed in the 1960s by behavioural scientist Paul Hersey and author Ken Blanchard in their book *Management of Organizational Behaviour* (1969). It is based on the nature of the relationship between the manager and their team. This relationship can take different forms according to the task, and the team's level of skill and motivation. If a manager can match their leadership style to the team members' fitness for work, this will enable the group to achieve their goals to the best of their ability.

Matching style to readiness

According to the Situational Leadership model, there are four management styles. Each has two aspects—task-focused or directed behavior and relationship-focused or supportive behavior—which are measured in different ratios, from low to high. At one extreme is "telling," based on clear, firm direction with less emphasis on support. In contrast, "selling" and "supporting" provide support for team members at different levels of competency. Finally, "delegating" allows a manager to step back and give team members freedom and responsibility.

> "People differ not only in their ability to do but also in their 'will to do'."
>
> Paul Hersey, 2008

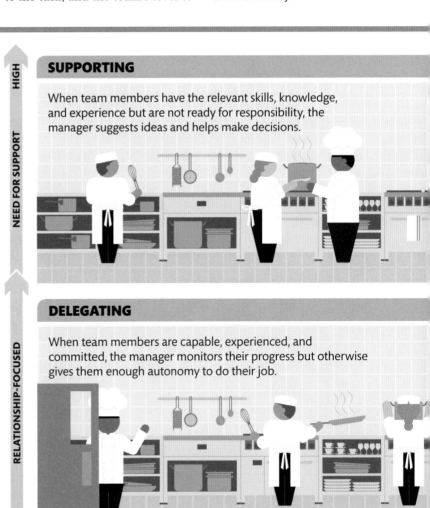

SUPPORTING

When team members have the relevant skills, knowledge, and experience but are not ready for responsibility, the manager suggests ideas and helps make decisions.

DELEGATING

When team members are capable, experienced, and committed, the manager monitors their progress but otherwise gives them enough autonomy to do their job.

NEED FOR SUPPORT

RELATIONSHIP-FOCUSED

HIGH

LOW

LOW

TASK-FOCUSED

Managers need to recognize each team member's level of competence and motivation. Hersey and Blanchard defined these characteristics as "performance readiness" and identified four such readiness levels (see below).

The underlying principle is that there is no single best style of leadership. Managers may have to adapt their approach in different situations, even for the same team members. For example, at the start of a new project or in a crisis, the manager may need to be more assertive, whereas later in a project, when team members have gained knowledge and experience, the manager may be able to take a more hands-off role. Successful managers are those who can adapt their style to match their team.

✓ NEED TO KNOW

> **The supporting style** is largely democratic; the team is given plenty of responsibility.

> **The selling style** is less democratic; the manager provides vision and direction.

> **The telling style** is autocratic; the manager gives clear, authoritative instructions.

> **The delegating style** is hands-off; the manager leaves the team to complete the job.

SELLING

When team members lack ability—perhaps due to lack of experience—but are enthusiastic about the job, the manager explains (or "sells") the task at hand and is available to give support.

TELLING

When team members lack skills and confidence, and may also be unwilling, the manager gives them precise instructions and closely monitors their progress.

ASSESSING THE THEORY

Like many management theories, Situational Leadership has been analyzed for its pros and cons:

Pros

> Easy to understand and apply.

> Enables manager to adapt leadership style to fit the situation.

> Focuses on maturity/competence of individuals and teams, often overlooked in considering effective leadership.

Cons

> Assumes people will always follow the leader.

> May not apply in all situations—for example, when time is short and tasks are extremely complex.

> May not work where managers hold a leadership position but act more as administrators or have limited power.

NEED FOR DIRECTION   **HIGH**

Management and Power

Many managers have power over people. However, there are different kinds of power, and a good manager knows which should be fostered and which should be avoided.

Power at work

With open-plan office floors and hot-desking, many of the traditional signs of management power, such as a private office, have now disappeared. However, people have more subtle ways to show their authority.

Power arises from a person's relationships with those around them. In work, different levels of power are formally defined in the organizational hierarchy. This kind of power may include the ability to reward or discipline team members. Other forms of power come from having specialist information or skills, being highly visible in work activities, or cultivating the right people ("office politics"). All forms of managerial power have their good and bad points; successful managers will moderate their power with fairness and self-restraint to direct and motivate their team.

Six sources of power

The effective use of power depends on the skills and character of the person holding power, their relationship with their employees, the task to be done, and the formal definition of management roles. Social psychologists John French and Bertram Raven identified five kinds of managerial power, with Raven later adding a sixth in his *Six Bases of Power* (2012).

Legitimate
This form of power comes with a position. The organization gives an appointed manager the power to direct the activities of their subordinates. Legitimate power can be granted, changed, or withdrawn by an organization and, as such, resides in the position rather than the appointed individual.

Reward
Power can be derived from the ability to control rewards that are valued by others. The greater the perceived value of such rewards, the greater the power. In business, such rewards include promotion and pay but also public recognition and praise.

Coercive
The opposite of reward power, coercive power is the ability to deliver punishments. These include demotion and dismissal but also psychological forms of bullying. While it can be effective in the short term, coercion tends to cause resentment and is often detrimental to performance.

The "gods" of management

Charles Handy, author of *Gods of Management* (1995), used ancient Greek gods to exemplify four management cultures based on particular roles and values. Each form has its advantages and shortcomings; managers may encounter different cultures in different companies, or even within different areas of one company.

Zeus: club culture
Power is concentrated in the hands of the top person, who exerts control through personal contacts rather than procedures (e.g., investment banks and brokerage firms).

Apollo: role culture
Power is hierarchical and clearly defined by job descriptions, with decisions being made at the top of the bureaucracy (e.g., life insurance companies).

Athena: task culture
Power is derived from the expertise required to complete a task or project, and decisions are made by meritocracy (e.g., advertising agencies).

Dionysius: existential culture
Organizations exist for individuals to achieve their goals, with decisions being made by the consent of the professionals (e.g., universities).

Expert
This kind of power is based on specialist skills and resides in the individual rather than their official role. A manager who is competent and knowledgeable is more likely to be respected by their subordinates; however, employees with expertise can also win respect and power too.

Referent
This form of power is derived from the trust and respect that a manager earns from their team and colleagues. Subordinates may come to model their own behavior and actions on those of the manager. It can take time to amass referent power, and a manager needs to understand the attitudes and culture of their team in order to build it.

Informational
Power can also be derived from the control of information. Informational power relates to specific situations, whereas other forms of power involve more general relationships. This type of power can be transitory: if the information is shared with other people, the power can be exhausted.

Scientific Management

Frederick Winslow Taylor introduced the idea of Scientific Management to the growing US manufacturing industry in the early 1900s. Today, his ideas still inform a great deal of management theory.

Working smarter

A mechanical engineer by trade, Frederick Winslow Taylor developed his ideas in the 1880s while working in a Philadelphia steelworks. He studied how his workers performed their individual tasks and evaluated how this affected productivity—a method that was later called "scientific" analysis. He summed up his findings in *The Principles of Scientific Management* (1911).His basic premise was that optimizing the way a task is done is more efficient than simply compelling employees to work harder.

Taylor did not value the human needs of workers, believing that they were motivated only by pay.

He argued that since workers do not naturally enjoy work, they must be closely supervised under an autocratic management style.

Analyzing tasks

According to Taylor, managers should separate production into a series of discrete tasks and find the best way to perform each one (in contrast to the widespread practice at the time, of workers devising their own "rule of thumb" methods). Workers should be given direction and training and the tools necessary for them to work as efficiently as possible. Finally, they should be paid by the number of items they produce in a set period of time, a

FOUR PRINCIPLES

Taylor's studies led him to devise four management principles:

> **Examine** each job scientifically in order to determine the "one best way" to perform the task.

> **Hire** the best workers for each task, and train them to work at maximum efficiency.

> **Monitor** each worker's performance, and provide instruction when needed.

> **Divide** the work so that the managers plan and train and the workers execute their tasks.

Case study: McDonald's

McDonald's is one of the largest fast-food brands in the world, selling 75 burgers every second. From Moscow to Marrakesh, the food looks and tastes the same. Every branch follows identical instructions for each stage of the process, from preparing, cooking, and packaging each food item to mopping the floor. The result is a triumph of Scientific Management and a vindication of Taylor's four principles (see box, left).

The responsibilities of managers and workers are kept separate. Managers oversee performance and quality, while workers deliver service on the front line.

practice now termed "piece-rate" pay. As a result, workers would be encouraged to work hard, maximizing productivity.

In the early 1900s, Henry Ford applied Scientific Management principles to car manufacturing.

He organized workers so that each executed a single task in the best possible way, and instead of moving around the factory, each worker remained stationary at an assembly line—an arrangement that

became standard for mass production. After World War II, Taylor's ideas influenced the kaizen philosophy in Japan, where the focus was on "lean production" as well as the elimination of waste (see pp.120–21).

McDonald's has mastered a consistent global system that ensures fast, clean, and reliable service. Production lines are standardized, with the use of machines that control ingredient amounts and cooking times to ensure high speed and high quality.

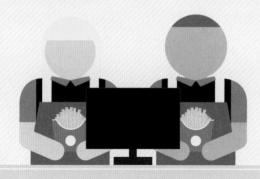

Recruitment and training are standardized, and corporate goals are advertised. The company even has a Hamburger University in Chicago.

A "pay-by-performance" philosophy provides long-term incentives. A recognition program, including an employee of the month prize, helps motivate staff.

"In the past the man has been first; in the future the system must be first."
Frederick Winslow Taylor, 1911

Key Principles

In 1916, French mining engineer Henri Fayol wrote his key principles of management based on what he considered fundamental truths. His work became one of the first guides for managers to be published, and it remains influential today.

Start of management theory

When Fayol published his groundbreaking *General and Industrial Management* (1916), which included his 14 principles—along with his five management functions (see pp.14–15)—rapid industrialization in Europe and the US meant that there was an urgent need for professional managerial techniques. His work soon became a widely used guide for managers, giving them the skills necessary to oversee increasingly complex organizations, and went on to form the basis of modern management theory. Although organizations, and how they are run, have changed significantly over the last century, the basic elements of Fayol's principles still apply. Tasks must be completed efficiently, discipline must be enforced, and staff must be rewarded. However, to get the best from their teams, managers today must apply the principles in accordance with modern working practices.

PRINCIPLE	SUMMARY OF PRINCIPLE	HISTORICAL APPLICATION	MODERN APPLICATION
DIVISION OF WORK	Assign specialized tasks to those workers with suitable skills.	Workers' roles became specialized to perform a single particular task.	Roles have become more generalized.
AUTHORITY AND RESPONSIBILITY	Provide managers with a level of authority that reflects their responsibilities.	Only managers held authority within an organization.	Employees are increasingly empowered.
DISCIPLINE	The organization must set clear rules/procedures for the manager to apply to workers.	The organization retained formal control over workers.	Rules/procedures now less formal, with increased peer-pressure control.
UNITY OF COMMAND	Workers should receive their orders from only one manager.	Workers always reported to a single manager only.	Teams may have multiple managers, particularly in matrix structures (see pp.54–55).
UNITY OF DIRECTION	There should be only one plan and one team performing functions with the same objective.	Each function followed one plan, overseen by a single manager.	Team structures and tasks are more complex and often have more than one objective.

PRINCIPLE	SUMMARY OF PRINCIPLE	HISTORICAL APPLICATION	MODERN APPLICATION
SUBORDINATION OF INDIVIDUAL	The organization's goals must take precedence over interests of individuals.	Employees were committed to the organization.	Organizations and workers are committed to each other.
REMUNERATION OF PERSONNEL	Compensation for work should be reasonable to both organization and worker.	Organizations adopted reasonable pay reward systems.	Rewards for workers may include feeling valued and respected as well as monetary gain.
CENTRALIZATION	Organizations must balance centralization and decentralization of authority.	Organizations adopted top-down decision-making, excluding worker involvement.	Management makes decisions on strategy; workers make decisions on specific tasks.
SCALAR CHAIN	The chain of authority and communication should be only formal and vertical.	Management structures became rigidly hierarchical with formalized communication channels.	Chains of command may vary from linear hierarchies to informal, flatter structures.
ORDER	Organizations must provide a safe workplace and resources in the right place, at the right time.	Internal information systems were used to control processes and workers.	Internal information systems are used for coordination purposes.
EQUITY	Managers should treat employees with equal fairness and respect to build commitment.	Organizations gained worker commitment through kindness and justice.	Worker commitment is built through a sense of shared ownership.
STABILITY OF PERSONAL TENURE	Organizations should give training and job security to reduce costly high staff turnover.	Organizations trained employees to encourage them to stay.	Organizations offer ongoing training and development so that workers choose to stay.
INITIATIVE	Organizations should employ only managers who can both conceive and implement new ideas.	Only managers came up with and implemented new ideas. Workers were excluded.	Many workplaces encourage free communication and ideas from workers.
ESPRIT DE CORPS	Managers must ensure that workers remain motivated and cooperate with each other.	Maintaining high morale within organizations became vital.	Group unity is less rigid; high morale comes from supporting individuals to give their best.

Global Management

As global business expands, managers who work across different countries have to understand their international markets and customers and grasp the complexities of differing standards, laws, cultures, and political systems.

A connected world

Thanks to modern technology, organizations increasingly span the globe, with employee and customer communication across many time zones. Managers at varying levels may have overseas responsibilities, from buying stock to controlling remote staff. Larger companies may have specialist managers, such as a business manager to further global efficiency and competitiveness, a country manager to handle all aspects of the local market, and a functional manager to nurture skills and transfer specialized knowledge—all overseen by a global manager to ensure coordination.

Whether working in-house or not, managers need to be aware of the business climate of the regions in which they operate. Those in touch remotely must ensure that local teams feel connected. Virtual meetings should be held at convenient hours, email communications must be clear, issues settled in a timely way, and all successes celebrated.

Culture and ideology

Studying the culture and beliefs of a country can help managers understand local business ethics and practices, which is useful when generating business and directing local teams.

Language

Good communications are essential. Hiring an interpreter to relay instructions may be necessary at times, and using expert translation technology can ensure that key documents are understood.

International finance

Managers need to know how monetary interactions between countries spanned by an organization affect profits. Fluctuating exchange rates may be a concern, as might currency controls that restrict the movement of money.

Managing internationally

Understanding the national culture, relevant laws, and local customs of countries within an organization's sphere allows it to run more smoothly, avoids falling foul of local rules and regulations, and ensures greater success. Sensitive handling of local issues can also be the key to securing new deals. Here are some pointers that managers should be aware of.

"The international manager reconciles cultural dilemmas."

Fons Trompenaars, cross-cultural theorist, 2000

CULTURAL SENSITIVITY

The ability to maintain good relations with a virtual team, or clients and business leaders in another country, is essential for a successful manager. To avoid mistakes, local customs and the nuances of different cultures must be understood. Small gestures can impress overseas clients and create a competitive advantage.

Language

Learning some phrases in the local language is polite and shows goodwill. Fluency—if resident long term—is even better. When speaking English, keep it clear to avoid misunderstandings.

Nonverbal communications

The index finger and thumb touching means "okay" in the US but is vulgar in Brazil. Pointing is offensive in many cultures. A nod may mean "continue" rather than "yes". (See Non-verbal communication, pp.172–73).

Customs

Mealtimes and eating habits—from making sounds when eating to the use of eating utensils—vary in different cultures. Specialty foods, from sea urchins in South Korea to grasshoppers in Mexico, may also cause confusion.

Time

Attitudes to time differ. While some countries are strict about time management, others are less so. In countries where people are more relaxed about schedules, negotiations may progress much more slowly.

Respect

There is no direct translation for the Chinese concept of *miànzi* (losing face). It is about a person's feeling of prestige and plays an important role in Chinese business. Understanding the idea is vital for working relationships in China.

Bureaucracy and regulatory standards

Business practices frequently vary between countries. Managers should know, for instance, if a local initiative needs government approval and must ensure compliance with local regulations on products and staff.

Political and legal systems

An awareness of the political and legal systems in different countries enables organizations to take advantage, for instance, of government incentives to invest and to avoid problems with differing tax codes or labor laws.

Time zones

Creating consistent schedules for contacting colleagues and teams in different time zones helps keep operations running efficiently. A mutually convenient social hour for virtual chats and catch-ups can boost morale and encourage goodwill.

Strategic Management

Strategic management is a continuous process by which managers establish an overall direction for an organization, specify objectives, and allocate resources to achieve their long-term goal.

Analyze, plan, execute

Before the 1960s, "strategy" was a term that related to warfare and politics, not business. Strategic management grew as a discipline through the work of management consultants such as Peter Drucker and Bruce Henderson, who recognized the need for a process that would take an organization from its present state to a more desirable one. The process starts with information and analysis and a crucial knowledge of external factors (see box, right), which together influence the formulation and implementation of a strategy.

Having identified options for an organization, managers can select long-term goals (a strategy) based on their understanding of the firm's capabilities. For the strategy to be implemented successfully, people across the organization who are best placed to have information about customers, competitors, and markets need to be involved.

Today, strategic management is an exciting field—globalization and technology are driving innovation and opening up opportunities for insightful, adaptable, and forward-thinking individuals.

Case study: Komatsu

Established in the 1920s, Komatsu is a Japanese manufacturer of construction equipment. After significant losses, it changed its strategic management approach at the start of the 21st century. By focusing on their key competitor, Caterpillar, and spreading a vision of global leadership, Komatsu's managers were able to encourage a desire to succeed among employees.

1 Create strategic intent

Having established the need for change, Komatsu's managers analyzed the situation, figuring out where the company wanted to be. To fulfill its ambition—to lead the market—Komatsu needed to "encircle," or take on, its main rival, Caterpillar.

2 Formulate a strategy

Next, the managers figured out how to achieve their long-term goal. Their strategy outlined how they would gain access to new customers, reduce costs, and enhance competitiveness, as well as spread business risk across a wider market.

3 Implement the strategy

The third stage in turning Komatsu's fortunes around was to implement the long-term strategy. Managers strengthened organizational and leadership capability and implemented the "Komatsu Way"—a set of values for employees to abide by.

OPERATING ENVIRONMENT

In the 21st century, strategic management has become ever more complex due to increasing numbers of external factors that can influence the operating environment and, therefore, strategic decisions.

External factors may include rapidly changing technology, environmental issues, geopolitical risk factors, and national and international differences in legislation—for example, while the use of plastic carrier bags in the UK attracts a small levy, in some countries, such as Bangladesh and Kenya, plastic bags are banned completely.

❯ **Global business** is being reshaped by disruptive technology (see pp.76–77), the shift from product- to customer-driven demand, increased automation, changes to the retail model with online shopping, and the ability to offshore or outsource work.

❯ **Concerns about climate change**, air quality, and plastic pollution have put sustainability high on the list for strategy considerations. Many manufacturers across the globe are rethinking their packaging, with the aim of making it recyclable and requiring fewer resources.

❯ **For worldwide business, geopolitics** must be considered because of risks such as terrorism, supply-chain disruption, and differences in how countries are governed.

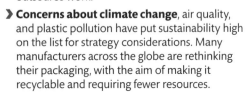

CATERPILLAR

330B

"**The essence of strategy is choosing what not to do.**"

Michael Porter,
US academic, 1980

4 Evaluate the strategy

Strategic management is an ongoing process, so Komatsu's managers continue to evaluate and innovate, measuring and improving the company's global systems in accordance with the mantra "success today does not imply success tomorrow."

Risk Management

Management is all about making decisions, and all decisions involve risk. By making a risk-management plan to define and analyze risks, managers can more easily cope with unexpected events.

Dealing with risk

Risks are inherent in every type of business or organization. They can range from natural disasters and accidents to legal liabilities, uncertainties in financial markets, or acts of sabotage by competitors.

The first step in creating a risk management plan is making a risk assessment (see box, right). First, all the risks known to an organization are listed. A weight is then assigned to each risk, based on the likelihood of it occurring and the level of impact it would have on the organization. The highest-weighted risks are prioritized and a plan is made to address them. The likelihood of a risk is never based on past performance alone but also on the extent to which the organization's environment has changed and is likely to change in the future. Risk monitoring—in the form of regular reviews, constant updating, and embedding risk management in organizational culture—is vital. It ensures that the manager and team can effectively address risks and identify opportunities.

The second part of risk analysis is risk-response planning (see below), in which managers and teams determine what action to take in response to a given risk.

✓ NEED TO KNOW

> **Many organizations** require risk assessments to be carried out by someone who is recognized as being competent to do so. The elements of competence can be expressed with the acronym KATE—knowledge, awareness, training, and experience.

> **To identify existing risks** and who might be affected, look at records of staff accidents (or near misses) or illness.

Mitigating risk

Risk-response planning helps managers decide whether to avoid, minimize, or accept a risk. There are three main elements: the context (risk environment); the assessment process; and how to monitor the effects of any action taken. This planning will enable a manager to allocate resources to negotiate the risks and communicate effectively with others involved.

RISK ENVIRONMENT

1. APPETITE
What level of risk is the organization prepared to accept?

2. GOVERNANCE
Is responsibility for the risk defined at every level of the organization?

3. PROCESS
Have procedures been established for identifying new and changing risks?

HOW BIG IS THE RISK?

Risks vary in importance, from minor, commonplace problems to rare but catastrophic events that can cause an organization to collapse or even endanger lives. A risk assessment is used to assign a risk-weighting for each issue by examining its likelihood and its impact on the organization. Risks with the highest potential for damage plus the greatest likelihood should be prioritized; the goal is to keep the likelihood and the impact of each risk as low as possible.

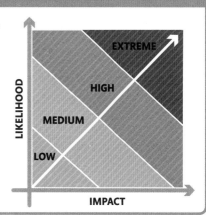

LIKELIHOOD

EXTREME

HIGH

MEDIUM

LOW

IMPACT

RISK ASSESSMENT

4. FRAMEWORK
Has a risk analysis been carried out to include all potential risks?

5. STRATEGY
What are the implications of the risks for the strategy of the organization?

6. MITIGATION
Have adequate processes been established to mitigate risks?

RISK MONITORING

7. METRICS
Can the value of the risk to the organization be measured?

8. ORGANIZATION
Have the risks been fully communicated throughout the organization?

9. CULTURE
Are risks being reported as an ongoing policy at all levels?

"It's impossible that the improbable will never happen."

Emil Julius Gumbel,
German mathematician,
1958

HR Management

Organizations need the correct human resources in order to deliver their products and services. HR managers help attract, train, and develop the right people in the right positions, but as worker expectations change, so does the HR role.

Changing role

The HR manager, or the manager playing an HR role, needs to recruit, train, appraise, and motivate staff, but the modern workplace has changed the way the role is fulfilled (see below). Traditional elements of the job remain: HR managers are still involved at every stage of the employee life cycle—from attracting and selecting the right talent to navigating the individual's departure. They must also manage issues such as safety, absence, and well-being. But shifting workforce models bring new challenges. In addition to pervasive change within organizations, employment patterns are also shifting. The gig economy—in which freelance workers are paid by each "gig" or job they complete—is growing.

Flexible and virtual working, and the blurring of boundaries between work and home life, alter team interactions. A workforce that is multigenerational, with different expectations and work ethics, adds another complex dimension, too. Managers are increasingly aware of the differing attitudes towards the growing pool of "millennials" (those born between 1980 and 2000), who will make up 75 percent of the global workforce by the year 2025. The HR manager needs to be aware and responsive to their expectations, such as a preference to work in teams, the importance of work-life balance, and the desire for rapid career development.

Reinventing HR

The role of HR manager has undergone a shift to become a much more proactive one. Managers are now expected to anticipate the company's staffing needs many years in advance, thinking strategically and developing existing employees.

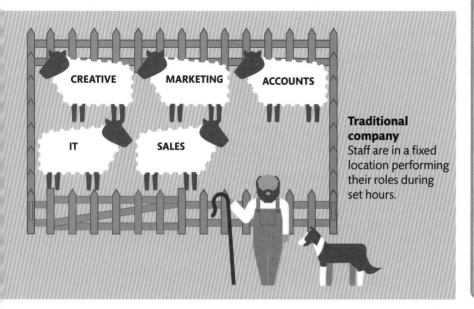

Traditional company
Staff are in a fixed location performing their roles during set hours.

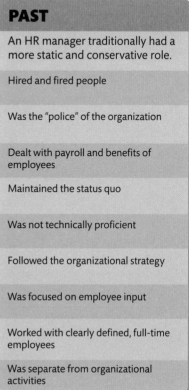

PAST

An HR manager traditionally had a more static and conservative role.

Hired and fired people

Was the "police" of the organization

Dealt with payroll and benefits of employees

Maintained the status quo

Was not technically proficient

Followed the organizational strategy

Was focused on employee input

Worked with clearly defined, full-time employees

Was separate from organizational activities

EMPLOYEE VALUE PROPOSITION (EVP)

HR managers must successfully engage employees. An EVP is the set of benefits a company offers that differentiates it as an employer. Benefits and financial rewards are no longer enough to attract and retain key talent and rank below other values, such as a career path and flexibility. At the apex of these values is a sense of pride and purpose.

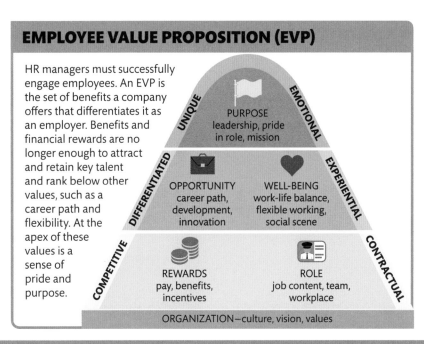

UNIQUE — EMOTIONAL

PURPOSE
leadership, pride in role, mission

DIFFERENTIATED — EXPERIENTIAL

OPPORTUNITY
career path, development, innovation

WELL-BEING
work-life balance, flexible working, social scene

COMPETITIVE — CONTRACTUAL

REWARDS
pay, benefits, incentives

ROLE
job content, team, workplace

ORGANIZATION—culture, vision, values

> "To make a living is no longer enough. Work also has to make a life."
>
> Peter Drucker, management theorist, 2012

PRESENT

An HR manager is now expected to develop staff more actively.

Engages and empowers people

Is thought leader and mentor of the organization

Promotes employee engagement and experience

Constantly challenges status quo

Is technically advanced, using big data and analytics

Shapes organizational strategy

Enables employee output

Unlocks potential in dynamic and changing workforce

Is integral to activities, communicating with staff to understand their needs

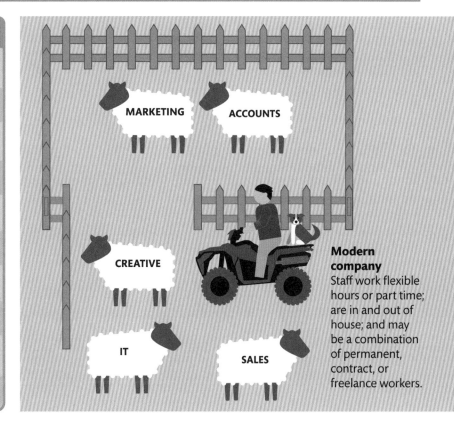

MARKETING

ACCOUNTS

CREATIVE

IT

SALES

Modern company
Staff work flexible hours or part time; are in and out of house; and may be a combination of permanent, contract, or freelance workers.

Financial Management

Finance is the lifeblood of a company. No matter how good its products or services are, the company will not thrive unless it is on a sound financial footing.

Staying afloat

All managers need to know about financial management, since most of their decisions will impact on company finances in some way. Financial management involves record-keeping as well as reporting, planning, budgeting, implementing financial controls, and ensuring that financial considerations are central to the decision-making process.

The primary concern of those managing finance in a company is how money enters the organization (through sales, fundraising, or financing—such as loans), and how money leaves (expenditure on materials, wages, distribution, and investments). In a small company, a financial manager will monitor this process, whereas in larger organizations the work is handled by a finance department. Whatever the company's size, its finance staff must keep an eye on the big picture and understand the potential short- and long-term impact of decisions. Looking after day-to-day expenditures is also crucial. Cash flow is a key indicator of financial health and something that finance staff must always monitor. A lack of adequate funds to pay essential bills, such as rent and wages, is the principal reason that operations fail.

Financing a new venture

Hannah is a financial manager in a small, privately owned furniture business. She is looking at a project to make chairs from recycled materials. There is demand for the environmentally friendly product and unused space in the factory. Here are some of the decisions she makes to ensure that the venture is profitable.

✓ NEED TO KNOW

> **Assets** are everything of financial value owned by an organization.
> **Liabilities** are everything owed, such as debts and loans.
> **Balance sheets** are snapshots of an organization at particular dates, listing assets and liabilities.
> **Profit and loss statements** are financial statements listing sales and costs; they are used to figure out gross and net profits.
> **The break-even point** is when total sales equals total costs.
> **The bottom line** is net income or total money earned after tax and other deductions.

1

IDEA

To manufacture environmentally friendly chairs from recycled materials.

5

FINANCIAL CONTROLS

Using risk management (see pp.32–33) and profit and loss statements, she assesses the venture's profitability in both the short and long term.

2
CAPITAL REQUIRED

Hannah calculates how much money is required to start production. This must include the factory space—an indirect cost, or "overhead".

3
CROWDFUNDING

To fund it, Hannah opts for online crowdfunding. She sets up the venture as a separate business and offers shares in return for public investment.

4
AGREES ON BUDGET WITH TEAM

Working with a project team, she schedules a detailed budget for the first 12 months of the venture, including the revenues from projected sales.

6
MANAGING THE FUNDS

Once the project is up and running, Hannah manages the withdrawal of money from the funding to meet costs, including the price of materials and salaries.

7
PAYING TAX

When the chairs begin to sell, she calculates any tax owed to the government on sales (such as VAT) and on profits.

8
ALLOCATING PROFITS

Since the business stays in profit, she calculates a fair dividend for her investors and reinvests the remaining profits in production.

Operations Management

Managing operations within a company involves planning, organizing, and improving the systems it uses to produce goods or provide services. In most larger businesses, this is a dedicated role.

Overarching role

Operations managers work across a broad range of sectors and industries. They focus on converting materials and labor into goods and services as efficiently as possible, using resources in the most effective way, to maximize profits. They manage the organization's core functions, whether in production, manufacturing, or service provision (when the product is not a physical object). Responsibilities may include day-to-day and strategic management that ranges widely across the organization's activities.

An operations manager involved in manufacture, such as in a pie factory (see below), would deal with the input of raw materials and oversee all the stages of production to the output of the product. An operations manager in a service business, such as an airline, would oversee processes—in this case, systems involving logistics and engineering.

Good operations management is key to a company's success, whatever the industry, and is one of the areas predicted to be transformed by artificial intelligence (AI) and automation, particularly in the service sector.

Managing a process

Sally is the operations manager in a factory making vegetarian pies. Her role involves coordinating labor and the use of raw ingredients. She ensures the pies are made, quality controlled, and labeled to exacting specifications then dispatched for distribution.

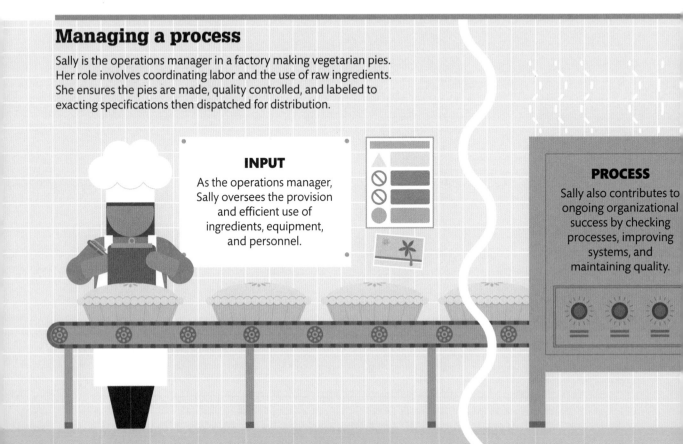

INPUT
As the operations manager, Sally oversees the provision and efficient use of ingredients, equipment, and personnel.

PROCESS
Sally also contributes to ongoing organizational success by checking processes, improving systems, and maintaining quality.

PRODUCT OR SERVICE?

For operations managers, the distinctions between manufacturing, where a physical object is produced, and offering a service, where no object is made, are not so clear-cut today. Many manufacturers now provide services with their products, and vice versa. New technology has further blurred the lines between manufacture and service; Amazon, for example, is a service provider, yet also makes, markets, and sells own-branded products.

MANUFACTURER	SERVICE PROVIDER
Tangible product	Intangible product
Inventory of stock	No inventory
Low customer contact	High customer contact
Long response time	Immediate response time
Capital intensive	Labor intensive

✓ NEED TO KNOW

> **Right first time** is the idea that avoiding mistakes in operations management is more beneficial and cost-effective than addressing problems after detecting them.

> **Effective capacity** is the maximum amount of work an organization can complete in a period due to constraints such as delays, material management, and issues of quality.

OUTPUT
Sally also bears responsibility for fulfilling orders to meet targets of time and cost.

SALLY'S PIES
SALLY'S PIES
SALLY'S PIES
SALLY'S PIES
SALLY'S PIES

Quality Management

Managers are responsible for ensuring that the quality of work produced by their team meets the required standard—whether they are manufacturing a product or providing a service.

Meeting expectations

People know good quality when they see it, and, typically, the higher the price a consumer pays, the higher the quality expected. A customer buying a car, for example, will expect the quality of a Rolls-Royce to be different from that of a Mini. For businesses, the key to successful quality management is ensuring the quality of their product or service meets or exceeds the expectations of their customers. Organizations manage quality control by setting standards and checking that these are being met at every stage of the process— for example, in manufacturing, when raw materials arrive in the factory, during production, and before the finished goods are dispatched to the customer.

Quality is everything

Traditionally, quality was managed through periodic inspections. If a defective product or poor service was detected at the time of an inspection, it was corrected— preferably before the consumer became aware of the problem.

Happy customer

Total quality management puts the customer first, defining quality as something that meets or exceeds customer expectations. People from across an organization are responsible for making sure these quality standards are met.

Quality standards are set according to customer satisfaction with the product or service offered.

Meeting set standards of quality is a continuous and organization-wide process.

Improvements to quality are driven by data and analysis, including customer feedback.

Today, quality management is at the heart of everything that goes on within an organization. Each process and activity is monitored to maintain a desired level of quality, and the focus is on exceeding customer expectations. This philosophy—that the long-term success of a business depends on customer satisfaction—is known as total quality management (TQM), and it originated in industrial Japan in the 1950s. All employees are committed to improving products, services, processes, and the culture of the organization itself.

ZERO DEFECTS

Philip Crosby came up with the idea of "zero defects" when he was a quality engineer at maufacturing firm The Martin Company in the 1950s. In his 1979 bestseller *Quality Is Free,* he wrote that quality is not about being bad or good but about meeting set requirements the first time and every time. Managers are responsible for setting standards and ensuring they are met. Crosby accepted that people make mistakes, but he argued that if organizations make allowances or expect things to go wrong, quality is more likely to be compromised. Problems should be prevented rather than cured.

✓ NEED TO KNOW

> **Crosby estimated** that organizations can lose 20–35 percent of their revenues by making allowances for defects or mistakes and the cost of rectifying them, rather than preventing the problems from occurring in the first place.

> **In setting clear requirements**, managers should view work as a series of processes that will result in predicted outcomes.

> **Improved quality** is likely to lead to increased profits.

Ensuring the customer is happy with the final product is at the heart of the organization.

Managers are responsible for the process of measuring quality against the set standards.

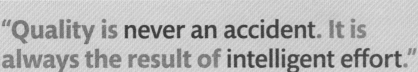

"Quality is never an accident. It is always the result of intelligent effort."
John Ruskin, 19th-century social thinker

IT Management

An information technology (IT) manager is responsible for monitoring a company's IT systems and resources, ensuring that they are up-to-date and cost-effective.

Technology in the workplace

The primary task of an IT manager is to ensure that the information systems of an organization are operating both effectively and efficiently. These systems include so-called "tangible" resources, such as computers, networks, mobile technology, and people, and "intangible" resources, such as software programs and data. In large organizations, IT managers report to a head of information, or chief information officer (CIO), who is likely to serve on the board of directors. As such, the CIO works at the heart of the organization, ensuring that any new initiatives have the required IT support.

Today, many IT managers are involved in digital transformation—the process of integrating new digital technologies into all aspects of a business. When digitization—the move from paper to digital—first happened, many organizations modeled their digital business on the previous paper-based setup. Increasingly, IT managers are choosing to replace traditional models such as company-owned hardware with cloud computing services. A key part of this process is anticipating the impact that these new technologies will have on the workplace of the future.

A changing world

IT is a rapidly evolving field, with innovations such as digital platforms (online businesses like Amazon and Airbnb), artificial intelligence, cloud computing (see pp.76–77), the Internet of Things (see box, below), and enterprise resource planning (using software to manage day-to-day business activities). In particular, digital technology has enabled organizations to capture and store vast amounts of sensitive data, making cybersecurity a growing concern and a key specialization in IT management.

Cloud computing

A third of a typical IT budget is spent on cloud computing services. These enable companies to store data and access computing power over the internet

THE INTERNET OF THINGS

One area changing the role of IT managers is the Internet of Things (IoT), or the embedding of technology in everyday objects. Smart home hubs already allow people to use their smartphones to control everything from lighting to kitchen appliances. Now, the IoT is transforming business, providing intelligent data and automation, creating demand for more skilled workers, and enabling remote working. IT managers face rising consumer expectations as IT becomes an integral part of products.

Data

Between 2016 and 2018, 90 percent of the world's data was created. A vast 2.5 billion gigabytes is now produced every day.

Artificial intelligence

Most IT managers agree that 20 percent of existing IT jobs will soon be replaced by AI but think that new jobs will emerge to make up for it.

New technologies

Digital technology is changing so rapidly that IT students are currently being prepared to do jobs that do not yet exist.

E-commerce

Projections show that by 2023, 22 percent of all retail sales will be made online. Without an online presence, a retailer is likely to fail.

IT teams

Although 71 percent of IT departments have a digital team, there is a shortage of key skills, such as big data analysis and cybersecurity.

In 2020, global spending on IT was an estimated

$5tn

International Data Corporation, 2020

DRIVERS OF CHANGE

According to a 2018 survey by research company Gartner, the role of the CIO is changing. IT delivery management now takes up less of managers' time, with new areas such as cybersecurity, big data, and artificial intelligence (AI) becoming increasingly important. The drivers of this change are digitization and technological innovation.

✓ NEED TO KNOW

❯ **Big data** refers to a volume of data that is so large that it is difficult to process using conventional analytical tools.

❯ **Cyberspace** is a virtual concept of the world's finite interconnected technology.

❯ **Business Intelligence (BI)** uses analytical technology to transform data into information to help with business decisions.

Marketing Management

Whatever the product, service, or cause being promoted, managers responsible for marketing need to be aware of consumer trends and use technology effectively to reach their target audience.

Getting the message right

Marketing is an essential function in any organization that sells products, provides services, or wants to make its voice heard. Larger firms may have specialist marketing managers, but in smaller companies, advertising and public relations may be combined in brand or product marketing roles.

The responsibilities of a marketing manager vary by sector but are likely to include conducting research, analyzing data, creating marketing campaigns, putting together social media plans, and coordinating team members to assist with these tasks. Digital skills are essential; technology and the global market have transformed marketing, and often the main sales channel is online.

When deciding how to promote and sell products, managers can draw on a wealth of digital tools to determine the target market, assess competitors, pinpoint trends, monitor customer responses, and predict future sales. However, customers also have digital power—online reviews make an impact—so marketing managers must keep up with social trends and concerns that might affect their sales.

On target

In a rapidly shifting, highly competitive world, the role of marketing manager is a dynamic one that requires customer insight and an expert awareness of trends. A manager can use various marketing tools to hit important targets. These tools must be used correctly, though; if mishandled, they may wreck campaigns and sales.

Big data analytics
Use the latest technology (including artificial intelligence to analyze large amounts of data) to uncover consumer insights and trends.

Customer lifetime value
Estimate the value of a customer's future sales potential to guide investment in marketing and loyalty programs.

Viral marketing
Encourage consumers to spread marketing campaigns via social media sites to reach a huge global audience.

Influencer marketing
Sponsor "influencers" on social media to promote products or services to their followers.

Subscription economy
Offer consumers access to products and services through subscription rather than purchasing.

MARKETING TOOLS

Positive customer feedback

Consumers can easily leave reviews online. Good reviews boost sales.

Trend awareness

Consumer values change rapidly. Organizations must maintain their relevance by keeping up with trends.

Sustainable approach

Consumers are becoming more environmentally conscious, so firms need to be seen to be green.

Clear branding

Customers buy into brands they believe in. A brand must stand out in a crowded marketplace.

Ethical policies

Many consumers prefer to deal with organizations that treat their staff and suppliers ethically.

Trust

Customers will deal only with organizations they trust, and companies can lose trust through poor service or misleading marketing.

MARKETING TARGETS

Direct marketing

Use highly targeted email and social media campaigns to pinpoint customers' interests and needs.

> "Consumers are seeking equilibrium in all aspects of their lives—between humans and technology, brand and personal, global and local."
>
> Pamela N. Danziger, marketing journalist, 2019

✓ NEED TO KNOW

> ❯ **Four Ps** (product, place, price, and promotion) are the key parts of a comprehensive marketing plan.

> ❯ **CTA** (call to action) is any marketing activity designed to prompt an immediate response or sale.

> ❯ **Inbound marketing** draws consumers to products and services via subtle branding, social media, and relevant web content.

> ❯ **Outbound marketing** targets customers via traditional channels such as television and billboards.

Digital Management

Digital technology offers great potential to develop new processes, products, and services, and ways of connecting with others—but it must be managed.

Embracing change

Digital technology is essential in most organizations and must be managed effectively. In some companies, it forms part of IT, while in others it is linked to marketing via the management of social media channels. Managers working in this field need to understand the potential of digital technology in order to make use of it across all areas of a company. This might include using social media to market goods or attract customers, for example, or analyzing data to find ways of increasing profitability.

A manager involved in formulating an organization's digital strategy, and who recognizes its role in the overall business plan, is better placed to initiate new technologies and explain their relevance to employees. Many teams are now multigenerational, and while some employees may struggle to keep up with the pace of digital change, those who have grown up in the digital age can adapt more easily. It may, therefore, be useful to break down traditional hierarchies by appointing digital leaders within a team to help implement change.

✓ NEED TO KNOW

> **Digital transformation (DX) is** the use of digital technologies to boost efficiency, accelerate processes, and create new business opportunities.

> **A digital strategy** is a company's action plan for applying digital technologies to enhance existing business activities. Managers have a vital role to play in its integration within an organization.

> **An ICT system** (information and communications technology) allows a company to process, store, and share quantities of data.

The digital world

Digital technology has reshaped daily life in the past 25 years. Millions of people work, shop, book vacations, play games, and listen to music online. Most communicate via cell phone rather than landlines, and nearly half of the world's population uses social media. Digital managers must embrace the opportunities this presents for marketing to an ever-increasing global audience.

Digital world

TOTAL POPULATION 7.676 billion

UNIQUE MOBILE USER 5.112

ACTIVE SOCIAL MEDIA USERS 3.484 bn

INTERNET USERS 4.388

> *"75% of global marketing spend will be on digital by 2021."*
>
> Jason Dent, Campaign Monitor, 2019

Global spend through digital channels

FASHION & BEAUTY

$524.9 bn

ELECTRONICS & PHYSICAL MEDIA

$392.6 bn

FOOD & PERSONAL CARE

$209.5 bn

FURNITURE & APPLIANCES

$272.5 bn

TOYS, DIY & HOBBIES

$386.2 bn

TRAVEL (including accommodations)

$750.7 bn

DIGITAL MUSIC

$12.05 bn

VIDEO GAMES

$70.56 bn

Global social media channels

	FACEBOOK	YOUTUBE	WHATSAPP	WECHAT	INSTAGRAM	TWITTER	LINKEDIN
WHAT IS IT?	Social media and networking service	Video-sharing website	Instant messaging application for smartphones	Chinese messaging, social media, and mobile payment app	Photo- and video-sharing social networking application	News and social networking application	Social networking site for professionals
ACTIVE GLOBAL MONTHLY USERS	2.41 bn	1.9 bn	1.5 bn	1 bn+	1 bn	321 m	303 m

(source: Service providers, 2019)

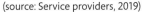

The Project Cycle

Aside from routine business, a company may also undertake projects, which are temporary and specific pieces of work that require management at every stage.

Overseeing projects

A project is a series of tasks created to achieve a particular goal. That goal could be to deliver a new product or service or a change in the business. Projects differ from ongoing daily tasks in that they have a start and finish and must be achieved within set limitations. Some projects are small, low-cost, and short-lived; others are vast multibillion-dollar undertakings that span decades.

A project manager is responsible for the day-to-day running of the project, organizing resources, and overseeing a team of people.

The manager must use a range of skills (see pp.60–61) to shepherd the project through each phase (see right) until the agreed goal is achieved, on time, and within budget.

A series of projects with related goals is termed a program. Each project in the program is headed up by a project manager, and they are all directed by a program manager, possibly a senior executive. On a large-scale project, the project manager may be overseen by a project board—a group of senior executives with a vested interest in the outcome.

NEED TO KNOW

> **A waterfall approach** consists of a detailed plan, a schedule, and handover of a completed project.
> **An agile project** is done in sprints and delivered in chunks.
> **Outputs** are the immediate deliverables from the project (usually a product or service).
> **Outcomes** are the wider changes the project delivers over time.
> **Scope** is the project's agreed output, outcomes, and benefits.
> **Scope creep** is the undesirable widening scope of a project.
> **The iron triangle** is the limitation of scope, cost, and time.

"Project management is the train engine that moves the organization forward."

Joy Gumz, Director of Project Auditors, 2012

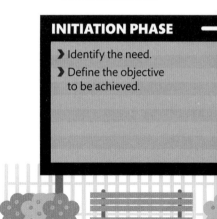

INITIATION PHASE
> Identify the need.
> Define the objective to be achieved.

Project phases
Projects are overseen by project managers and move through initiation, planning, delivery, and handover phases

The program
A series of projects makes up a program, which is kept on track by a program manager.

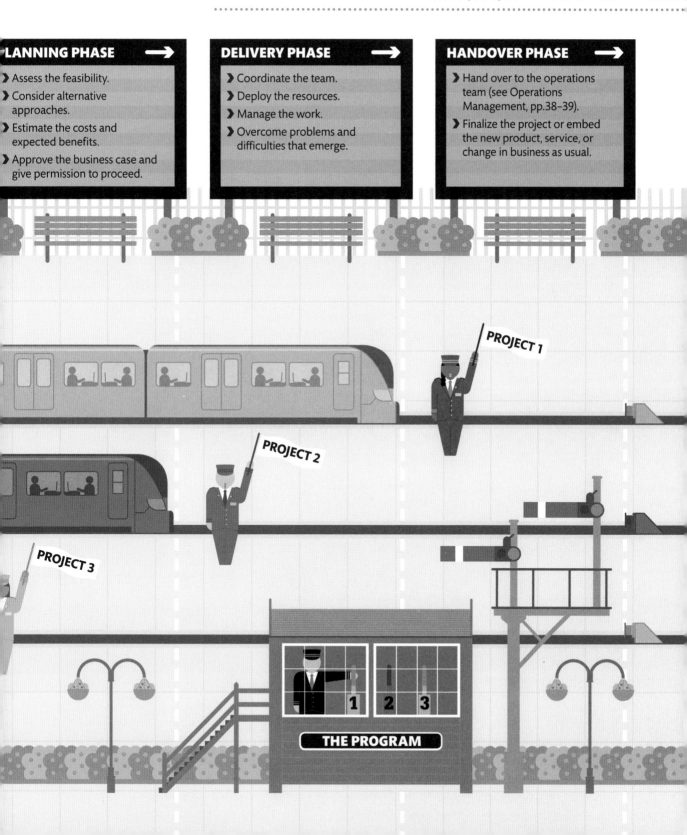

PLANNING PHASE →

- Assess the feasibility.
- Consider alternative approaches.
- Estimate the costs and expected benefits.
- Approve the business case and give permission to proceed.

DELIVERY PHASE →

- Coordinate the team.
- Deploy the resources.
- Manage the work.
- Overcome problems and difficulties that emerge.

HANDOVER PHASE →

- Hand over to the operations team (see Operations Management, pp.38–39).
- Finalize the project or embed the new product, service, or change in business as usual.

PROJECT 1

PROJECT 2

PROJECT 3

1 2 3

THE PROGRAM

MANAGING ORGANIZATIONS

Types of Organization

Companies do not operate in isolation. Managers need to understand the different types of organization that they are likely to encounter, since these can become future partners, clients, competitors, or customers.

Different sectors, different objectives

Organizations fall into three main categories: privately owned companies that seek profit for individuals or shareholders; government organizations that serve the public interest; and nonprofit bodies, such as charities and community-run projects. Whichever sector a manager works in, overseeing employees, maximizing efficiency and productivity, and setting and meeting targets are central to their role. Just as profit-driven companies expect the largest possible return on an investment, so public and nonprofit bodies strive for the best possible outcomes from their initiatives. As such, a successful manager may find their skills in demand regardless of the sector they work in.

While their objectives vary, organizations within different sectors commonly collaborate to share their expertise or resources on joint projects and enterprises. For example, a private company may be contracted by a government body to perform public services, while a charity may provide specialist knowledge to both. However, conflict can also arise between organizations, such as when a private company opposes a government objective or a charity campaigns against the actions of a private company. In order for their own organization to succeed, it is essential that managers are able to collaborate effectively with other agencies when necessary, while also being aware of the potential for conflicts and having the skills required to resolve them.

Today, organizations are constantly changing, and the lines between different sectors are becoming less distinct. Public-private partnerships between businesses and governments are now commonplace, while many larger charities have commercial operations. For a manager, this trend offers a wealth of opportunities.

PUBLIC SECTOR
This includes government-funded bodies that provide public services. They do not operate for profit but seek value for money on their expenditure.

Shared assets and risks

Collaboration across sectors is increasingly widespread and can involve multiple organizations and complex relationships. Each partner will be aiming to get something different out of the relationship, and this may be a source of conflict unless the relationships are managed carefully. Similarly, although each organization will aim to contribute assets and expertise to a joint venture, they may also bring an element of risk to the other partners. For example, when the privately owned UK facilities and construction conglomerate Carillion PLC collapsed in 2018, the UK government lost £180 million as a result of their public-private partnership. The collapse also stalled major public infrastructure projects.

PRIVATE SECTOR

This includes organizations that are owned by individuals or shareholders. The enterprises range from single traders to international conglomerates. All aim to make a profit for their owners/investors.

20%

how much less a PPP can cost a government vs. a traditional design-bid-build model

DJ Gribbin, founder of Madrus LLC

PPPs

A public-private partnership (PPP) is a contract between a government body and a private company to provide a service or asset. The company expects to make a profit.

JOINT PROJECTS

Many nonprofit organizations collaborate with public and private enterprises to secure funding, access resources, or raise their public profile.

NONPROFIT SECTOR

This sector includes organizations that are owned by trusts, such as charities and public initiatives. They use any money gained to fund their activities and to pay their employees.

Evolving Structures

The structure of an organization determines where decisions are made, and the ultimate purpose of structure is to satisfy the customer in the most efficient and effective manner.

Types of structures

There are numerous structures within an organization and between organizations, and many companies are having to restructure to keep up with changes in the working environment. Increasingly, they are moving away from traditional hierarchical structures (see right) and creating flatter ones, such as matrix structures (see far right), to speed up decision-making. Temporary collaborations are also becoming more common, in the form of virtual organizations (see above right).

A traditional business has two broad functions: a delivery function, which includes research and development (R&D), sales and marketing, and operations and supply; and a support function, which includes finance, information technology (IT), and human resources (HR). Each function is typically broken down into departments run by a departmental head, and these are further divided into teams overseen by managers. This means that a traditional business structure is hierarchical, featuring a series of reporting relationships and a vertical chain of command. Team managers, for instance, report to their departmental manager, who reports to the directors, who report to the CEO. Even conglomerates, which are made up of multiple, unrelated businesses, usually have a parent company, the CEO of which has influence over its subsidiaries.

> **"To survive in modern times, a company must have an organizational structure that accepts change as its basic premise..."**
> Ricardo Semler, CEO of Semco Partners

However, not all organizations have a simple hierarchy. In matrix structures, the strands of reporting are set up as a grid. Staff are typically organized into teams responsible for project delivery, reporting to a project manager, but are also linked to a particular discipline or department (for example, engineering), and so must report to a functional manager as well.

Hierarchical structure
A traditional business structure is a hierarchy of reporting relationships, with a CEO at the top, followed by directors, then managers, and then teams reporting in at successively lower levels.

VIRTUAL ORGANIZATIONS

A virtual organization is a network of independent organizations that are brought together, often temporarily, to produce a product or service. One example of this was the UK Government's Project Leadership Programme. Three separately managed entities—Cranfield University, PA Consulting, and The Project Academy—pooled their teaching, coaching, and IT resources and facilities to deliver a development program for civil servants.

Matrix structure
In a matrix structure, staff have two lines of reporting: to a functional head and a project manager. This system enables staff to work on a range of short-term projects while retaining links with their functional department.

THE STAR MODEL

American organizational theorist Jay Galbraith created the star model to explain why so many organizations fail to improve their performance by changing their structures alone. He thought that structure should be guided by an organization's strategy, or long-term goals, and that it should also be integrated with organizational processes (how information is distributed), rewards (motivating employees to embrace the strategy), and people practices (having the right workforce to take the organization in the desired direction).

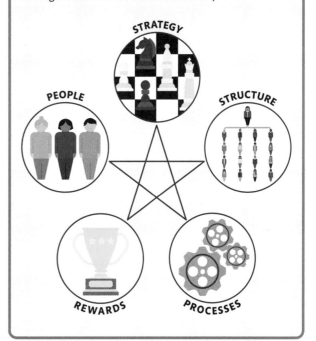

✓ NEED TO KNOW

❯ **Organizational structure** determines how an organization is managed. It describes the hierarchy of decision-making, where each employee's job fits within the overall system and how information is passed between reporting levels.

❯ **A vertically integrated company** is one that owns its supply chain and manages every stage of its product. This enables it to adapt swiftly to change.

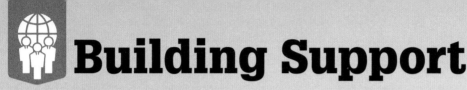

Building Support

Defining what an organization stands for—its purpose, values, and ethics—plays an essential role in enlisting the support and cooperation of employees, customers, and clients.

Making statements

To be successful, managers need their staff and the external parties they deal with to support their organization's strategy. This means that the organization must appear to be relevant—it must stand for something that people can believe in and work towards. An effective way for managers to achieve this is through a mission statement. This is a public declaration that explains what the organization does and why. Mission statements should be engaging and easy to remember; for example, Google's reads: "To organize the world's information and make it universally accessible and useful."

To support a mission statement, managers may also produce a vision statement. This presents an image outlining where the organization aspires to be in the future—its long-term goals—based on achieving its mission. Typically emotive in tone, a vision statement describes the journey the organization is on, which the manager wants people to buy into. To this, a values statement can be added, which then explains the values the organization will uphold while on that journey. These values usually include moral, ethical, and environmental pledges, such as how it will treat employees, suppliers, and natural resources.

Collectively, these statements form a pledge between the organization and those it deals with. It is therefore important that the promises made are attainable and actively pursued.

Focusing attention

The advantages of a mission statement are twofold for the manager. When viewed externally, it forms part of the organization's image and brand and serves to attract like-minded people, such as employees, clients, and investors. It also reminds existing stakeholders of what it stands for. Internally, it is an effective way to reiterate the organization's strategy to employees, encouraging them to work toward it. It also helps remind employees of the organization's commitment to them, promoting trust. For the manager, an effective mission statement creates a guiding light for and within the organization they run.

MISSION STATEMENT
This is what we do,
what we are,
and why we do it.

CASE STUDY

Uber Technologies, Inc.

Founded in 2009, Uber sought to reinvent private-hire transportation with its simple taxi-hailing app. As an upstart in an established industry, it needed to attract drivers and customers to its platform.

> **Mission statement** "Transportation as reliable as running water, everywhere for everyone."

> **Vision statement** "We ignite opportunity by setting the world in motion."

> **Values statement** "We do the right thing. Period."

"OUR ORGANIZATION IS RELEVANT TO YOU—WE SHARE YOUR BELIEFS."

"Why do you exist as a company? What's the really compelling reason why you exist?"

Jørgen Knudstorp, CEO Lego, 2017

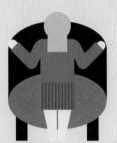

VISION STATEMENT

This is where we want to be in the future—it is the journey we are on.

VALUES STATEMENT

This is our promise of how we will treat people and the planet while on our journey.

Workplace Culture

The culture of an organization is a reflection of its personality. Developing and sustaining a positive workplace culture can greatly improve morale and attitudes among staff.

The right culture

The culture of the workplace arises from everything that happens within the organization. Internally, culture influences how staff interact with each other; their productivity and how motivated they feel; and how they treat customers and clients. It is also evident externally, either directly, in how the organization seeks to present itself, or more indirectly, through the reputation arising from its actions. Many factors can influence an organization's culture (see below), not all of which may be within a manager's direct control, such as decisions made at a more senior level or where the company is located. However, as much as possible, a manager should work to develop a culture that best suits their area of responsibility.

For example, a manager in a high-tech business, where success depends on rapid decision-making and innovation, might foster a very different culture from one in a regulatory body, where checking facts and carefully considering policy is paramount. A manager should also consider the needs of their staff, because people respond to different cultures in different ways. The culture to avoid, however, is a negative one.

Creating a culture

An organization's culture evolves over time and is influenced by many factors, such as its values, how staff are managed, and even its working environment. Managers must understand these factors in order to effectively shape and maintain the desired culture.

CULTURE

Culture is a combination of numerous factors that can create a positive and productive working environment or a negative one.

Practices

How an organization conducts itself can influence how employees feel about working there.

Place

The working environment provided for employees can have positive or negative effects on staff morale.

TYPES OF ORGANIZATIONAL CULTURE

In the 1990s, Charles Handy—an Irish management theorist and authority on organizational behavior—defined four distinct types of workplace culture (see pp.22–23). Based on power, role, task, or people, each culture has different strengths and weaknesses for the organization and may suit some personnel better than others. For a manager, it is important to understand the type of culture that is present in their organization and to shape or harness it to best suit their staff, goals, and objectives. It is also essential to communicate any cultural change to staff and encourage them to buy into it.

POWER CULTURE
A small number of people hold power and influence. Decisions are made quickly and bureaucracy is reduced, but the organization is heavily dependent on the abilities of those in charge. Staff without power may feel excluded and demotivated.

ROLE CULTURE
The power and influence an individual can have is determined by their role within a rigid structure. Decision-making and adapting to new circumstances can be slow. Ambitious staff who value results and control over their work may feel frustrated.

TASK CULTURE
Organizations with a task culture depend on the unifying power of group working. Personnel are selected for finite projects and then redeployed to work where their expertise is most needed. Staff must be flexible and adaptable.

PERSON CULTURE
Everyone has power—the organization exists to allow skilled individuals to achieve their own objectives. This type of culture is typified by specialists or consultants who can operate with a degree of autonomy within an organization.

Values
Employees and stakeholders may feel motivated by the values an organization upholds, such as ethical standards.

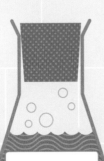

Vision
An organization's vision—its goals and how it sees itself (see pp.56–57)—should be reflected in its culture.

Leadership
The leaders of the organization exemplify the culture and should set an example to staff and the outside world.

People
To have a coherent culture, the majority of people working in the organization must share the same values.

Managing Projects

To successfully oversee a project, managers need the skills to deal with the constraints of scope, time, quality, and budget, while also effectively leading a team and communicating with stakeholders.

Keeping a project on task

A project life cycle has several phases (see pp.48–49) and a project manager must effectively manage each of these so that the work is delivered on time, on budget, and to specification. This demands close control of procedures, strong teamwork, and clear communication to all stakeholders. A manager will also need to troubleshoot problems, such as a slipping schedule, as they arise (see box, right). All these challenges require a range of hard and soft skills (see below). Hard skills are technical ones that can

be readily acquired. For instance, a good project manager should be able to produce a workable schedule that includes interim goals and tools such as key performance indicators, enabling them to monitor work and keep it on track.

Soft skills are interpersonal ones, such as good communication. This is a key skill for managers, who will need to regularly share information with clients, higher management, and team members who may be from different organizations, have diverse disciplines, or work in multiple locations.

Balancing act

Successful project management involves efficiently managing schedules, risks, financial resources, relationships, individual and team input, and a range of stakeholders. To achieve all these objectives, project managers need a combination of hard technical skills and soft people skills.

"75%
of long-term job success depends on people skills, while only 25% on technical knowledge."

Peggy Klaus, business author, 2008

Hard skills

These are technical skills that are easy to measure and to teach. They include defining the goals of a project, scheduling and budgeting, managing risk, and selling.

PLANNING · TIME MANAGEMENT · BUDGETING · SELLING · RISK MANAGEMENT

OVERCOMING OBSTACLES

Every project manager is faced with challenges at some stage. The table below shows some commonly encountered problems and gives suggestions on how they might be tackled. These obstacles include an unclear vision at the start of a project, falling behind schedule, scope creep (a change to the objective), and an unrealistic deadline.

	Problem	Solution		Problem	Solution
	UNCLEAR VISION	• Seek clarity from senior management/stakeholders • Review initial objective • Ensure team is clear on the direction and avoids stalling		SCOPE CREEP	• Assess requests for change against business case/project objectives • Negotiate to align any change with project plan
	SCHEDULE SLIPPING	• Revisit timeline and reassess interim goals • Map out remaining work and assess risks to customers		UNREALISTIC DEADLINE	• Brief stakeholders and staff on likely impact of new deadline • Find out reason for delay • Adjust expectations • Identify most critical tasks

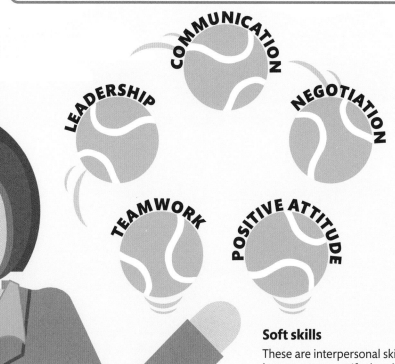

COMMUNICATION

LEADERSHIP

NEGOTIATION

TEAMWORK

POSITIVE ATTITUDE

Soft skills

These are interpersonal skills that are less easy to quantify than hard skills. They include the ability to lead, to create a vision and inspire a team, to communicate, to negotiate, to have a positive attitude, and to motivate and coach a team.

✓ NEED TO KNOW

❯ **A Project Initiation Document (PID)** enables managers to set out the business case for a project, establish the scope, size, and duration of the task, predict any possible risks, and plan a timeline for the work.

❯ **Project planning methods** help managers set clear objectives.

❯ **Key performance indicators (KPIs)** enable managers to see how closely they are meeting goals such as remaining on schedule and controlling costs.

Customers and Other Stakeholders

In order to balance the demands and expectations placed on an organization, a manager needs a clear understanding of the people who use its products and services and those who have an interest in, and effect on, the business.

Why stakeholders matter

An organization's stakeholders are vital to its success. Stakeholders are those parties that have an interest in the organization, such as its owners, shareholders, employees, and suppliers, and also includes the customers who buy or use its products and services. Managers must be able to identify all the stakeholders in order to understand what each group needs and wants from the organization. This allows managers to balance the interests of the various stakeholder groups with those of the company.

At times, the interests of one group may conflict with those of others. For example, increasing pay will please employees but will push up costs, resulting in a price rise that will upset the customer. Trying to please both parties by paying the rise and also keeping the product price low could then affect profits, resulting in a lower return for shareholders or owners. Hence, a balance must be struck between these opposing needs, remembering that whatever action is taken may have consequences for other stakeholders.

The bigger picture

In any organization, there is a host of stakeholders – internal and external – whose interests matter because they all contribute to the success of the business. To make decisions that benefit all parties, managers – who are themselves stakeholders – must know who these groups are and understand their concerns.

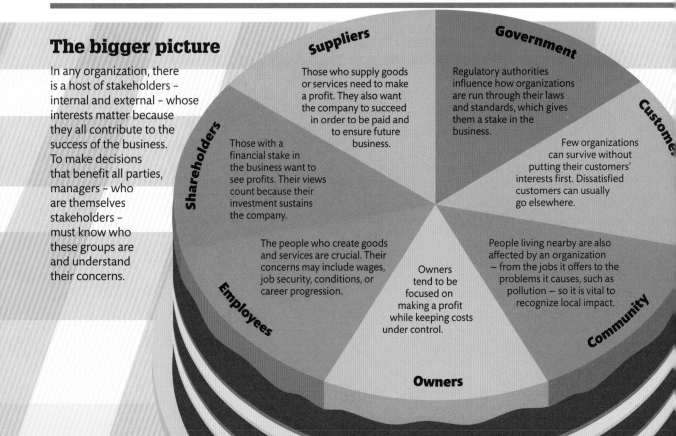

Suppliers
Those who supply goods or services need to make a profit. They also want the company to succeed in order to be paid and to ensure future business.

Government
Regulatory authorities influence how organizations are run through their laws and standards, which gives them a stake in the business.

Customers
Few organizations can survive without putting their customers' interests first. Dissatisfied customers can usually go elsewhere.

Shareholders
Those with a financial stake in the business want to see profits. Their views count because their investment sustains the company.

Employees
The people who create goods and services are crucial. Their concerns may include wages, job security, conditions, or career progression.

Owners
Owners tend to be focused on making a profit while keeping costs under control.

Community
People living nearby are also affected by an organization – from the jobs it offers to the problems it causes, such as pollution – so it is vital to recognize local impact.

In some organizations, larger stakeholder groups may consist of subgroups, often referred to as "segments," which have their own needs. Shareholders, for example, may include a segment of large institutional investors, such as pension funds, who might expect dividends (regular financial returns from their shares). A different group of smaller investors may prefer to see the value of their shares increase so that they can sell them at a profit.

"Stakeholder mapping," usually a graphical representation of the interests of key stakeholders, can help managers make decisions—for example, when planning a project or developing a marketing strategy.

SATISFYING STAKEHOLDERS

Customers are essential stakeholders in most organizations, although identifying who the customers actually are is not necessarily straightforward, as this example demonstrates. Here, the manager of a pet food manufacturer balances the needs of the company with those of the customer.

MANUFACTURER

The manufacturer wants to sell their pet food for the best price to the retailer, whose broader needs must also be satisfied.

RETAILER

The retailer wants to buy the food at the lowest price and sell it for the highest, while meeting the needs of suppliers and customers.

PURCHASER

The customer wants to buy nourishing food at a reasonable price that their dog will enjoy. The customer can shop elsewhere.

CONSUMER

The dog can eat only the food that is provided. If it does not like the food, the customer will want to find an alternative brand.

Manager
The manager wants the organization to prosper while balancing the demands of all stakeholders.

"To keep everyone invested in your vision, you have to... really analyze who the different stakeholders are and what they individually respond to."

Alan Stern, former NASA executive, 2011

Products and Services

In recent years, advances in digital technology have changed the nature of products and services. However, the overall objectives of managers involved in these industries remains the same.

Evolving markets

Traditionally, a "product" was a physical item that could be bought and owned, and a "service" was an activity performed for a buyer. Nowadays, however, the distinction between the two is not so clear. Fifty years ago, a record company could specialize in producing vinyl records and distributing them to main-street shops, whereas today most music is distributed as a download in digital format. This means that record companies have not only reduced the number of physical, "tangible" products that they produce—in favor of "intangible" digital products—but they have also adapted to new forms of distribution. This follows a more general trend, in Western economies at least, of consumers preferring experiences to things—a fact that has led to a flowering of

Tangible and intangible

In recent years, there has been a huge shift toward intangible products. People used to buy records, cassettes, and CDs, whereas today consumers tend to download music as digital files. Both the product and the service have changed, marking a shift from the physical to the digital, and from the main street to the internet.

> "Being on par in terms of price and quality only gets you into the game. Service wins the game."
>
> Tony Alessandra, author and marketing expert, 2009

Tangible products
Traditionally, music was available only as a tangible product that could be bought and sold on the main street

Intangible products

Today, music can be downloaded from a variety of websites. It is purely electronic and can be accessed almost anywhere.

the service sector and a decline in manufacturing. This shift from the tangible to the intangible, and from products to services, has had an impact on all sectors of industries. Many energy companies no longer see themselves as suppliers of electricity and gas but rather as providers of heating and lighting, which has enabled them to develop associated products and services.

Nevertheless, the objectives of organizations that offer products or services remain unchanged. For a private-sector company, the product or service must make a profit for owners or shareholders. Managers in charge of any part of the creation and delivery process monitor its efficiency, which is measured by how well money, labor, and materials are converted into products or services. Quality is the responsibility of a quality assurance manager, whose role it is to ensure that the product or service meets a certain standard. If it fails to do so, the organization can face the immediate wrath of its customers, not least in the form of damaging online reviews.

NEED TO KNOW

> **The sales funnel** is the entire sales process, including marketing, from initial contact with a customer to final sale.

> **A bill of materials** (BOM) is a list of all the components necessary to build a product or service.

> **A product tree** or product structure tree is a visual device that product managers often use when considering all the elements a product or a service may require.

> **"Feature bloat"** is a derogatory term used to describe a product that has too many features.

"Retro" revival
Although the internet offers a vast choice of music, old-style tangible products are currently enjoying a revival.

CASE STUDY

Rolls-Royce

In the 1990s, Rolls-Royce replaced its product-based business model with a customer-based model. It did so because its aeroengines were becoming ever more durable and so were selling in fewer numbers. In response, it expanded its limited maintenance and repair service, which saw profits rise from £300 million in 1993 to £1.2 billion by 2002. In the same year, it launched Rolls-Royce CorporateCare®, which offered maintenance at a fixed price for each hour its engines were in the air, plus access to lease engines during maintenance. This profitable service benefits clients by making maintenance costs predictable and removing any risks related to unexpected events.

Supply and Demand

The law of supply and demand explains the relationship between sellers and buyers. A manager must understand this fundamental concept in order to ensure that their business runs profitably.

Abundance and scarcity

For centuries, the law of supply and demand has been central to Western capitalism. Essentially, it states that there is a price at which buyers are prepared to buy and at which sellers are prepared to sell. If there is a scarcity of a product or service that people want, people will pay more for it and suppliers can therefore charge higher prices. However, if there is an abundance of supply with plenty of competition, people can choose whom they buy from, and so suppliers have to charge less. If other suppliers see that they can charge more for some products, they may decide to enter that market, creating more supply. Buyers will then have more choice, so prices will drop accordingly.

Supply hinges on factors such as available skills and raw materials, production technology, and the cost of labor, while demand is affected by consumer preferences and influences such as competing products, consumer incomes and needs, and seasonal fluctuations.

Managers must monitor and balance both supply and demand to regulate output and prices to their benefit. This requires continuous analysis of not only sales but also market trends and forecasting and planning for future demand.

> ## "price... does not depend on merit but on supply and demand."
>
> George Bernard Shaw, *Socialism*, 1926

High supply/low demand
A vendor who has a large stock of fruit and little demand can lose money because they have to sell the fruit off cheaply since it cannot be stored.

A balancing act

This market fruit stall illustrates some of the key factors in supply and demand. A vendor must ensure that they have a regular supply of good-quality produce from one or more reliable growers. However, if they stock too much for the demand, they may have to reduce prices to avoid wasting the fruit, reducing their profits. If demand is high and they cannot meet it, customers may either look elsewhere or be prepared to buy less and pay more if the fruit is generally scarce. The goal is to achieve a state in which supply and demand are roughly in balance.

ETHICS AND THE LAW OF SUPPLY AND DEMAND

The law of supply and demand suggests that people will buy more of a product they consider to be excellent value for money. This has led to the development of fast-moving markets that provide goods at very cheap prices. One example of this is the fast-fashion industry. In order to produce low-cost clothing, some retailers have resorted to sourcing garments from manufacturing sweatshops, where workers are housed in poor and sometimes dangerous conditions and are paid low wages. However, there has been a backlash against this practice. Several well-known brands have been "named and shamed," with the result that some customers are boycotting their products, despite the low prices.

✓ NEED TO KNOW

> **A free market** is a largely unregulated economic system in which prices for goods and services are determined by supply and demand.

> **A monopoly** occurs when a supplier or organization controls enough of the market to force a change in price.

> **Price fixing** is an agreement between competitors to sell a product at a set price—lower, higher, or its current level. In some markets, this is considered illegal.

High demand/low supply

A vendor who does not anticipate demand and has too little stock loses money, which affects profits and consumer confidence.

Balanced supply and demand

Managing the supply of seasonal produce correctly, while also assessing both present and future demands, keeps the business in equilibrium.

Marketing and Selling

Effective marketing is essential in any organization that sells products or services or has a cause to promote, such as a charity. It requires a knowledge of the customers and their needs, and how to reach them.

The marketing process

Marketing is a complex process that involves identifying a need, developing a product or service to meet that need, and promoting it to potential customers. The product should be offered at a price that people will pay and accessible from suitable outlets, and the buying and owning experience should be as positive as possible. For the manager, this requires researching markets to find opportunities and learning what customers need from the product, what they will pay, how they would prefer to access it, and what they will expect from the product itself and the organization offering it. In addition, the manager must identify the best way to promote the product.

Although the exact steps a manager will take to market their product will depend on what they aim to sell, market and customer research is essential. Developing a detailed strategy is also vital to ensure that the marketing process reaches the right audience and encourages it to buy the product.

Marketing in action

One of the most widely used theories about effective marketing that covers the whole process is "The 7 Ps," which refers to product, price, place, promotion, physical evidence, process, and people. This theory was proposed in its modern form as the "4Ps" in E. Jerome McCarthy's *Basic Marketing* (1960). Another marketing concept, of debatable origin, is AIDAS—attention, interest, desire, action, and satisfaction. Both theories are demonstrated in the scenario shown here.

Identify a market
The first task is to research a market and identify a need that is currently unfulfilled by existing products and services. What do people need?

Develop a product
Having identified a need, a *Product* (which includes services) should be developed to satisfy it, to be sold a *Price* that customers will pay.

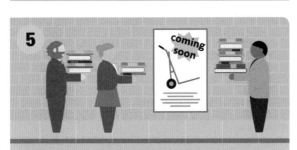

Capture attention and interest
Customers must be made aware of the Product and its benefits through advertising or *Promotion* that captures their *Attention* and inspires *Interest*.

Encourage action
Customers need to *Desire* the Product before taking *Action* and buying it, perhaps through incentives, such as a discount.

> "Marketing's job is never done. It's about perpetual motion. We must continue to innovate..."

Beth Comstock, Former CMO & Vice Chair of General Electric, 2014

THE VALUE OF BRANDING

Customers commonly feel more confident buying products and services from brands that they like or have an affinity with. For the customer, a brand embodies the identity and values of the whole organization, which it should seek to maintain. For the organization, its brand values should underpin every aspect of how it deals with its customers. This extends to the quality of its products, how and where they are made available, and how customers are treated at the point of purchase and beyond.

✓ NEED TO KNOW

❯ **Search engine optimization** is a digital tool, used to make an organization's website easier to find on the internet.

❯ **Targeted marketing** involves pinpointing the specific needs of a market and tailoring the sales message to that market.

❯ **Inbound marketing** is the process of attracting customers via compelling internet content.

❯ **USPs,** or unique selling points, are the qualities of a product or service that make it different from those of the competition.

3

Plan a marketing campaign
With a market identified and a Product developed, a marketing strategy should be planned based on the original research to ensure it is effective.

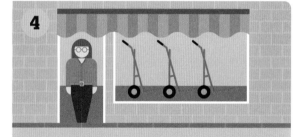

4

Determine place
The Product must be made available to customers through appropriate outlets, or *Place*, at the right time and in sufficient quantities to meet demand.

7

Sell product
Every step of the buying process, from advertising to final purchase – the *Physical evidence* – must give the customer confidence in the Product.

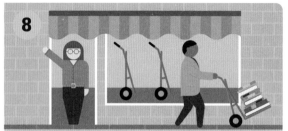

8

Ensure customer satisfaction
Customer *Satisfaction* is vital. It will be influenced by how the customer is treated by the business at each stage – the *Process* – and its staff, or *People*.

Winning Deals

Managers always aim to strike the best deal, but this should never be done at the other party's expense. Far from being a one-off transaction, a successful deal is the basis of a sustainable working relationship.

Negotiating success

To manage effectively, winning is not simply making a fast deal and moving on. According to Stanford University professor Joel Peterson, successful negotiation is more of a conversation in which both parties work to resolve a problem (see pp.188–189). To broker such deals, both parties must consider the other's interests at all times. People tend to dislike being sold things but do like to have their needs met. This means listening rather than talking so that everyone's needs—especially considerations of scheduling—are clearly understood. Preparing well so that the pricing reflects good value for what is being offered is also important. For these reasons, being honest

Prisoner's Dilemma

Ideally, people should work together to achieve a win-win. However, game theory—a field of study in which applied mathematics is used to analyze how parties make interdependent decisions—shows that this is not always the case. In the "Prisoner's Dilemma", an imaginary scenario posed by US researchers Merrill Flood and Melvin Dresher in 1950, two rational people are unlikely to cooperate, even if it appears to be in their best interests. Two criminals are held separately for a crime. If each betrays the other, they each face two years in jail. If one stays silent while the other betrays them, the traitor goes free, while the other receives three years in jail. If both stay silent, they each receive one year in prison. Collectively, it would be best for both to keep quiet. But both players will make the move that is best for them individually, but worst for them collectively: they are both likely to betray each other.

Prisoner A talks
For talking to police and betraying Prisoner B, A is jailed for 2 years.

Prisoner B talks
For talking to police and betraying Prisoner A, B is jailed for 2 years.

Prisoner A stays silent
Despite staying silent, Prisoner A is betrayed by B and is jailed for 3 years.

Prisoner B talks
For talking to police and betraying Prisoner A, B is set free.

and authentic in negotiations, and striving to ensure that solutions are fair, are key parts of deal making.

Open, constructive negotiation is especially important given the human inclination to compete rather than cooperate. Economists model this tendency in the form of the Prisoner's Dilemma, which shows that the best result for a group is never achieved by self-interest alone (see below).

CLOSING A DEAL

Being skilled at closing a deal is vital. A meeting can go well for all parties, but unless an agreement is reached, the deal is not done. Follow-up meetings may be needed to reach a point where a deal can be agreed on, ideally face-to-face or on the phone. At this point, one party should summarize all the points of the deal and ask whether the other is ready to agree. It is then vital for the active party to stay silent, which forces the other to respond. In the perfect scenario, both parties agree to the deal, but if one raises any qualifying conditions, the other should ask further questions to resolve issues. With goodwill, good deals can be done.

"Trust is the lubricant for successful business transactions."

Joel Peterson, 2018

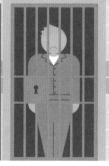

Prisoner A talks
For talking to police and betraying Prisoner B, A is set free.

Prisoner B stays silent
Despite staying silent, Prisoner B is betrayed by A and is jailed for 3 years.

Prisoner A stays silent
For staying silent and refusing to betray Prisoner B, A is jailed for 1 year.

Prisoner B stays silent
For staying silent and refusing to betray Prisoner A, B is jailed for 1 year.

Strategic Thinking

An organization's strategy—the vision of where it wants to be in the future—should always be at the forefront of a manager's mind, influencing every aspect of their daily decision making.

Developing strategy

Strategic thinking is a vital aspect of a manager's role. It identifies long-term goals and determines how to achieve them. Tools for strategic thinking include SWOT analysis, which can be used by managers to identify strengths, weaknesses, opportunities, and threats (see pp.104–105). The PESTLE framework is an effective method of analyzing wider external factors (see below), while the Boston Matrix focuses on internal capabilities (see box, below right). Together, these tools can be used to build strategies that are both wide-ranging and adaptable.

PESTLE

The PESTLE (political, economic, social, technological, legal, environmental) tool is an effective way for managers to analyze the external factors that affect an organization. It ensures that all decisions are based on reality rather than wishful thinking. Ideally, managers should communicate the resulting strategy throughout the organization and review it regularly to keep it up to date. There are many variations on the PESTLE analysis, which bring other factors into play.

Political (P) and Economic (E)

Evaluate the political and economic climate. How might operations be affected in countries with which diplomatic relations are strained? What is likely to happen to exchange rates or inflation?

Organization

Social (S) and Technological (T)

Gauge the impact of social and technological factors on the organization. Is the demographic demand for products or services growing or declining? Can technology be used to streamline operations? Do technological advances pose threats or bring opportunities?

WHO CREATES STRATEGY?

Strategy used to be considered the sole responsibility of senior managers, but Canadian academic Henry Mintzberg argues that strategy can arise from any level of an organization. The more people that managers can involve at each level, the greater the number of ideas and the stronger the commitment to them. But strategy is not just for the organization as a whole—each managerial unit, function, or department needs a strategy.

NEED TO KNOW

> **Strategy** focuses on a manager's long-term goals.
> **Tactics** concern the short-term actions that managers need to take in order to reach long-term goals.
> **On the difference** between strategy and tactics, Chinese strategist Sun Tzu observed: "Strategy without tactics is the slowest route to victory. Tactics without strategy is the noise before defeat."

"Know yourself and you will win all battles."

Sun Tzu, Chinese military strategist, c.5th century BCE

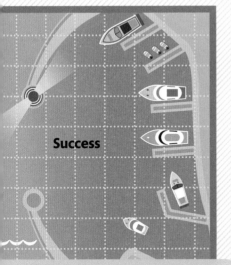

Success

Legal (L) and Environmental (E)

Examine the legal and environmental context. Will future legislation or regulatory change affect the organization? Does the organization have a firm environmental strategy, and do its activities comply with sustainability requirements?

THE BOSTON MATRIX

Developed by the Boston Consulting Group in 1968, the Boston Matrix can be used by managers to set strategies for products, services, or functions. Those that are classed as "Stars" should be invested in, since they are high growth and have a high market share. "Cash cows" should be milked, since they are low growth but have a high market share. "Question marks," on the other hand, deserve further analysis, since they have the potential for high growth but currently enjoy a low market share. Finally, "Dogs" should be sold off, since they are low growth and have a low market share.

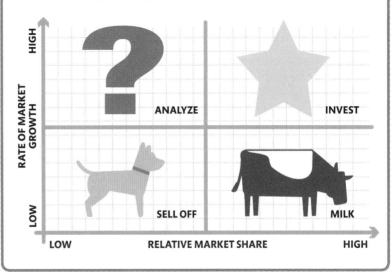

Effective Planning

Successful organizations are the result of in-depth planning, not luck. To get to where it wants to be in the future, an organization must map out the course it will take and all the stages involved along the route.

Planning for success

To achieve any goal, resources—such as time, money, people, and equipment—must be identified, sourced, and then allocated efficiently. Managers should prioritize tasks according to importance and establish a timeline for completion. By instituting monitoring processes, managers will be able to evaluate progress towards the goal and ensure that the goal is achieved in the desired time period. As part of the planning process, managers need to embrace uncertainty, preparing possible alternative courses of action to prevent the plan from being derailed by future events. Having a clear plan will encourage buy-in, help staff to feel that they are all working towards a common goal, and facilitate better understanding and communication between everyone involved.

Four types of planning

To run an organization successfully, a manager needs to plan in both the long and short term. The broadest, most far-reaching form of planning is strategic planning, in which important external factors, such as potential market changes, are evaluated against the organization's goals. The most extensive form of strategic planning is scenario planning, in which a number of possible future situations are considered and assessed (see box, right). Tactical planning is then used to identify the specific actions that must be taken. The most immediate form of planning is operational planning, whereby the manager details the way the organization functions on a daily basis, such as how it makes its products or delivers its services. However, no amount of forward planning can prevent unseen challenges, and it is essential that managers develop contingency plans for each planning stage, in order to keep the organization on track.

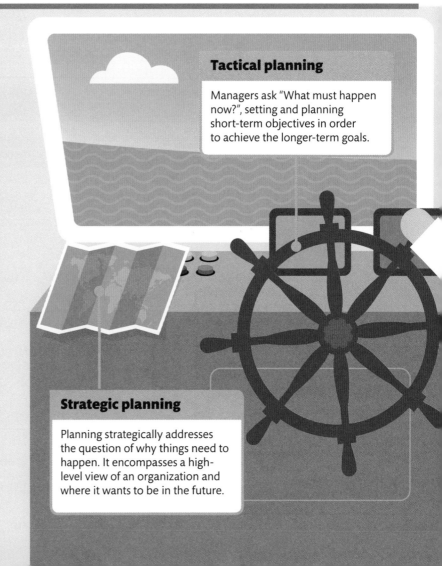

Tactical planning

Managers ask "What must happen now?", setting and planning short-term objectives in order to achieve the longer-term goals.

Strategic planning

Planning strategically addresses the question of why things need to happen. It encompasses a high-level view of an organization and where it wants to be in the future.

CASE STUDY

Royal Dutch Shell

The value of scenario planning was recognized by Royal Dutch Shell in the 1970s, when the oil market was highly volatile due to the formation of the OPEC cartel of oil-producing nations. Shell had begun using a "What if?" approach to plan for potential scenarios in the 1960s, which left it better prepared than its rivals to weather the economic storm. The company continues to plot "Shell Scenarios", including planning for a low-carbon future, along with increased water and food insecurity.

"Scenario planning is a discipline for rediscovering the original entrepreneurial power of creative foresight in contexts of accelerated change."

Pierre Wack, developed scenario planning at Royal Dutch Shell, 1985

Operational planning

Planning the operational, day-to-day aspects of an organization involves formulating an ongoing plan of what needs to happen and how it should be done.

Contingency planning

Planning for contingencies involves preparing an alternative course of action that can be followed in the case of unexpected events.

SCENARIO PLANNING

The aim is to consider different ways in which the future might unfold, and the impact of each scenario on a particular issue. The rule of thumb is to develop at least four "What if" scenarios to get a broad range of outcomes. However, variables based on data such as demographic trends are more reliable than those based on speculation—for example, about future economic conditions.

Disruptive Technology

Every organization relies on technology, whether for basic communication or as part of a manufacturing process or service provision. However, as technology evolves it brings both opportunities and threats.

Taking a leap

Updating technology is an essential part of ensuring that an organization operates effectively and remains competitive. However, it is equally important to anticipate how evolving technology may impact on the organization's products and services in the future.

Technology usually develops incrementally, through continual improvement, as seen in the steady evolution of the automobile. However, sudden leaps also occur, such as the advent of digital photography, which replaced film in the early 2000s. Such sudden and unforeseen new products, referred to as "disruptive technology" by US academic Clayton Christensen, have the power to reshape whole industries. Established products and brands can rapidly become obsolete, while fledgling start-ups may become global giants.

For a manager, disruptive technology can affect their organization in a number of ways. First, it has the potential to make any technology currently used

New ways of workings

Cloud computing—the hosting of software, files, and information online—illustrates the impact that disruptive technology can have for managers. In the past, the vital data and programs used by an organization was held on individual computers and local servers, which meant that most employees who used them were essentially deskbound. With these resources now online, staff can access everything they need via the internet, allowing for far greater flexibility in how, where, and when they work. Outside the workplace, the cloud is also revolutionizing daily life through "smart" devices, known as the Internet of Things (see pp.42–43). Connected togther via the cloud, these give users remote control over the technology in their homes, making life yet more flexible.

Work life before the cloud

Employees are restricted to work hours at set locations, using a local server. The capabilities of mobile devices, such as smartphones, is limited to the amount of data they can store.

outmoded or even redundant, resulting in the need to invest in replacements—particularly if competitors rush to be early adopters. While the organization will benefit from having the latest technology, it can also cause disruption within the workplace, as new practices are implemented and staff trained. Secondly, disruptive technology can sideline the products an organization manufactures or supplies, which can undermine its very existence unless it is able to innovate or find alternative markets for its goods.

In order to benefit from—or prevent the damage caused by—disruptive technology, a manager must stay alert and be willing and able to respond accordingly. However, they should first scrutinize any new innovation and assess whether to adopt it—as it may itself be soon surpassed—or to wait until it becomes more established.

There is no clear answer to this, which serves to illustrate how disruptive such sudden changes can be to an organization.

CASE STUDY

Apple and Netflix

Apple and Netflix are both good examples of disruptive start-ups. Apple made the leap from existing technology that utilized computers as merely tools for handling documents and created entirely new ways of using them. Netflix attacked the video rental model in 1997 by sending DVDs by mail and then disrupted the its own model by offering on-demand online video streaming, attracting 151 million subscribers by the end of 2019.

Cloud computing

The "cloud" is an internet space that enables users to store and access data using remote servers instead of a local computer's hard drive.

Mobile new world

Being able to access and store software and data online allows for mobile working. Smartphones become as capable as desktop computers.

MODEM

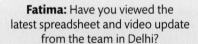

Fatima: Have you viewed the latest spreadsheet and video update from the team in Delhi?

Matteo: Yes, I am looking at the spreadsheet now. I will export it as a PDF and attach it to the sales brief.

Fatima: Fantastic, do you have time to edit the video before we meet?

Matteo: OK, although I will need to update the app on my phone first.

Fatima: If you are free tomorrow, can you join me in a video conference with the managers in Germany?

Matteo: No, sorry, I am working for another client at home tomorrow, all day. I will check my schedule.

Organizational Learning

For an organization to thrive, its managers need to foster a culture of learning. Learning through experience and sharing the resulting knowledge will ensure continuous improvement and development.

Learning to improve

In times of change, managers and employees must be prepared to adapt rapidly. For example, they may need to respond to what their competitors are doing or to a new technological development. The ability to change quickly and build capability is greatly enhanced by learning—and the impact on an organization's success is far greater if managers can establish a culture in which everyone is creating, acquiring, and sharing knowledge.

For learning to flourish, managers need to nurture a supportive environment that enables people to learn from mistakes rather than be blamed for them. Employees should be encouraged to voice opinions and be valued for the contributions they make. This can be facilitated by a flatter management structure, with fewer lines of reporting, which makes it easier for managers to hear individual voices. Managers should communicate clearly and openly, allowing staff at all levels to understand what is going on and put mechanisms in place to ensure that information is shared, not kept for personal advantage.

Senge's five disciplines

Peter Senge popularized the concept of the "learning organization" in his 1990 book *The Fifth Discipline*. It refers to an organization that facilitates learning and uses that learning for continuous transformation. Senge's five principles, or "disciplines," are useful to managers trying to establish a culture of learning. The fifth discipline is systems thinking, which integrates the other four.

"Through learning we become able to do something we never were able to do... we extend our capacity to create..."

Peter Senge, *The Fifth Discipline*, 1990

MENTAL MODELS
The thought processes that underlie a person's perception of what is happening and how things work can be positive or negative. A good manager will help expose them.

PERSONAL MASTERY
An individual's commitment to learning and to applying that learning is known as personal mastery. Managers should encourage team members to learn rapidly and continuously.

HOW PEOPLE LEARN

Different people learn in different ways. Managers need to take these "learning styles" (see pp.208–209) into account and offer a variety of learning opportunities to employees.

Some team members will learn best in a group situation, for instance, while others may prefer to perfect their skills through private practice before presenting them in public.

PRACTICE
Practicing in a low-pressure environment can help people perfect what they are doing.

FORMAL TRAINING
Taking a course or being sponsored through college will suit certain employees.

LEARNING FROM OTHERS
Watching other people and gaining from their experience can reinforce learning.

GROUP LEARNING
Discussing ideas and openly reflecting on and learning from them can be invaluable.

TEACHING OTHERS
Teaching others forces the teacher to think more deeply about their own knowledge, giving them insight.

SYSTEMS THINKING
The understanding that an organization is made up of interdependent parts that must work in harmony. This can help managers assess learning across all parts of their organization.

TEAM LEARNING
Listening, learning from others, and sharing best practices are key to shared learning. Managers need to create an atmosphere of trust to enable this to happen.

SHARED VISION
A shared vision provides a focus for motivation and learning. Managers should encourage employees to embrace the company's vision.

Market Forces

Economist Michael Porter identified five competitive forces that act on every industry. His Five Forces model enables managers to assess the ability of their organization to overcome that competition.

The nature of competition

One important influence on the success of an organization is the competition—the number and activities of rivals that provide similar products or services. It is therefore important to know what your competitors are doing. In the 1970s, Michael Porter took the concept further by defining other competitive forces in addition to rival firms. His article "How Competitive Forces Shape Strategy," published in the *Harvard Business Review* in 1979, illustrated how awareness of these wider competitive forces can help managers understand their organization's position in the marketplace and so move toward one that is more profitable and less vulnerable to attack.

Porter identified five forces that influence an organization's ability to attract and effectively serve its market and ultimately make a profit. His Five Forces model is sometimes represented as a cross-shaped structure. Existing competitors—the most obvious force—are placed at the center, surrounded by the four other forces. The bargaining powers of buyers and of suppliers form one pair of complementary forces, placed at opposite sides of the diagram. Potential new entrants and substitute products form the other pair of forces.

Flying into turbulence

Porter's model can be clearly applied to the airline industry. The strength of all five forces makes the airline business fiercely competitive, with low profit margins. Established rivals all compete on price and customers can easily search for the best deal. Suppliers, such as manufacturers or airports, take much of the profit. New players often offer low-price fares. Substitutes are available in other forms of transportation: trains, buses, and cars.

Bargaining power of suppliers
Those who supply a scarce or valuable resource, with few alternatives, can demand higher prices.

BLUE OCEAN STRATEGY

Blue Ocean Strategy (BOS) is a marketing theory and title of a book by W. Chan Kim and Renée Mauborgne. BOS states that a company is better off searching for uncontested marketplaces instead of competing in existing ones. The idea is to create and capture new demand, making the competition irrelevant. A good example of BOS is Netflix. The firm created uncontested marketing space by loaning movie and TV shows over the internet, something that no one else was doing at that time (see p.76).

Threat of new entrants
New firms can win market share from existing companies, but their power is limited by barriers such as expertise.

SOFT DRINKS

In the soft drinks industry, market forces are relatively weak. Big brands limit the threat of substitute products by ensuring wide product availability: for instance, installing branded vending machines so that competitors cannot offer their products in the same places. By contrast, the Dr. Pepper brand minimized its vulnerability by avoiding the top-selling cola segment, maintaining a narrow flavor line and marketing extensively.

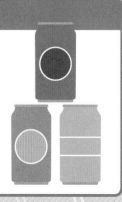

Rivalry among existing competitors
The number and strength of rivals can squeeze profits, but a distinctive brand identity can help a firm win market share.

Bargaining power of buyers
Powerful buyers, or those with multiple choices, can exert pressure to lower the prices they pay.

Threat of substitute products or services
If a similar or more attractive product is available elsewhere, it can reduce prices.

"The key to growth—even survival—is to stake out a position that is less vulnerable to attack from head-to-head opponents."

Michael Porter, *Harvard Business Review*, 1979

Gap Analysis

Comparing present performance with what was intended, and analysing the difference—the "gap"—between the two, enables managers to identify and address weaknesses within an organization.

Managing improvement

A form of strategic planning, gap analysis begins with evaluating the current "state" of a manager's area of responsibility by comparing the actual situation with what was expected or desired. This reveals any missing or weak strategies, capabilities, or resources. By comparing the current state with the target state, the manager can decide what steps need to be taken in order to bridge the gap.

Gap analysis can be used in a range of different management settings—from personnel management to budgets and scheduling—and to assess many different issues. For instance, when an athletic club's membership drops and it misses its subscription targets, or there is a marked fall in the quality of coaching it delivers, gap analysis could help identify and implement more effective administrative and athlete-development systems. Or when a dairy farm regularly runs short of animal feed, it could point to improvements needed in stock management systems. If some members of a team are performing better than others, gap analysis could help identify best practices.

Closing the gap

Gap analysis is a four-step process that can be used to give immediate and long-term improvements. In order for it to be successful, a manager must understand the organization's current position and set clear, measurable objectives for the future.

PRESENT
Low efficiency and weak profit margins

ISSUES-BASED PLANNING

An alternative evaluative tool to gap analysis, issues-based planning is most effective when applied to internal problems. It is well suited to managers in young or resource-poor settings where multiple issues are faced and involves:

> **Identifying** pressing issues, such as insufficient funding or low customer satisfaction.

> **Agreeing** on action plans—including who is responsible for each task—to address each issue over the next 6–12 months.

> **Executing** the action plans and regularly tracking progress.

Once the issues have been resolved, a broader, more complex strategic planning model can be adopted.

"To be successful, your personal plan must focus on what you want, not what you have."

Nido Qubein, President, High Point University, North Carolina

1. Identify area of analysis and goals to be accomplished: establish which management functions are failing and identify measures to reverse the trend.

2. Establish current state: analyze quantitative data—such as employee turnover and rates of equipment failure—and qualitative data, such as customer feedback.

3. Define future state: project a realistic target for employees that is achievable and will enable the organization to function effectively and successfully.

4. Bridge the gap: compare current state with future state and identify measures that will help get back on track.

THE VRIO FRAMEWORK

To help determine the internal strengths and weaknesses of an organization, a manager may use the VRIO framework. This tool is used to identify the organization's competitive advantages by asking four questions about its resources and capabilities. Do they add *value* and enhance overall performance? Are they *rare* and in demand? Are they *imitable* and therefore difficult for competitors to copy? Are they sufficiently *organized* within the organization? This insight can then be used as part of a gap analysis or separately to refocus the organization's strategy.

FUTURE
20 percent increase in efficiency; 25 percent increase in profits

Benchmarking

Benchmarking is a technique that managers can use to enhance the performance of their team or company by studying successful rivals, making comparisons, and initiating improvements.

Setting standards

Understanding how other teams or organizations succeed is an important tool for any manager. Benchmarking, as this is known, enables managers to identify any weaknesses in their own business by comparing key aspects of it with those of leading rivals.

When using this technique, a manager must first determine an appropriate benchmark—a rival team or organization whose success they wish to mimic. They should then study that benchmark by looking at its performance—comparing specific areas, such as product quality, customer satisfaction, or profitability. The manager should also look at the processes it uses, such as how it produces and delivers its products or services. Finally, the manager should explore the benchmark's organizational strategy and any

best practices it employs that might underpin its success. Having studied the benchmark, the manager then needs to apply what they have learned to their own situation and implement plans for improvements.

The process

The exact process that a manager will follow when benchmarking depends on the nature of their organization, the nature of the competition, and the purpose of doing the benchmarking. The most important steps are identifying the weakness in their own organization; setting a realistic benchmark; and researching the gap between the two organizations. Once an action plan has been decided, it should be reviewed to ensure that the outcomes are being met.

Internal review

When used within an organization, benchmarking allows a manager to make comparisons at all levels—between departments, teams, or individuals. Again, the objective is to identify the strengths in one and

Assess weaknesses
Rahul, a professional dog walker, has few clients. He fears that his own dog's scruffiness may be deterring them.

1

Establish a benchmark
Rahul compares his dog to a competitor's, whose pet gives a much better impression to clien[t]

2

Gather data
Rahul also conducts research to discover how best to improve the appearance of his dog.

DOG GROOMING

OPEN

4

Develop a plan
Based on his research, Rahul decides on a detailed plan to improve his dog's appearance.

5

9

9

the weaknesses in the other, which should then be addressed. This process is especially useful for companies that operate in multiple regions, or produce a portfolio of goods or services. The technique can also be used to determine the best practice in areas such as marketing, finance, and human resources, establishing ethical standards, as well as when considering new technology.

NEED TO KNOW

> **A benchmarking gap** is the difference between a company's performance and that of its target benchmark. The manager should aim to bridge this gap.

> **The "best in class"** is the highest standard achieved in a particular industry. It sets the benchmark for other companies.

CASE STUDY

Formula 1

The world of Formula 1 motor racing is highly competitive, with just fractions of a second making the difference between winning and losing. Reducing the time taken during pit stops is therefore critical. In 2012, it took the best teams around 2.4 seconds to change all four wheels on a racing car. This time has since been reduced dramatically, partly by teams meticulously studying what the fastest ones are doing and how they are doing it. Today, four wheels can be changed in less than 1.9 seconds.

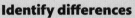
Identify differences
Having set a benchmark, Rahul establishes what would make his dog more appealing.

3

Action and monitoring
Rahul enacts his plan and has his dog groomed, which attracts new clients. He now ensures his pet is always kept clean.

6

"I still work hard to know my business. I'm continuously looking for ways to improve all my companies."

Mark Cuban, US entrepreneur and billionaire, 2011.

Sustainability

A sustainable business is one that has a positive impact on the environment and society. Many businesses are weaving sustainability into their strategy, realizing that doing good is not only right but also wins over investors.

Operating responsibly

Far from being a new concept, operating responsibly has been part of management for centuries. In the late 1800s, US piano maker George Steinway built a rural site near New York to house workers. His intention was "to give the workingmen a chance to live as human beings ought to live." In the 1890s, George Cadbury built Bourneville in the UK to provide a good life for workers at his family-owned chocolate factories. Both men realized that people work better if they are happier and believed in the responsibility of employers to improve their workers' lives.

A new strand emerged in the 1960s, when the environmental movement drew attention to the harm inflicted on the natural world by human activity. More recently, public dissatisfaction with poor conditions for workers in the developing world has pressured organizations to take responsibility for their actions and has increased support for initiatives such as Fairtrade. The drive for sustainable practices has also come from business—a World Economic Forum survey identifies environmental risks, such as extreme weather, as a major concern.

Weighing the cost

To ensure that an organization prioritizes sustainability and that it satisfies all relevant environmental laws and regulations, a manager should focus on four key principles. These ensure that the use of resources is assessed, agreed upon, monitored, and made public.

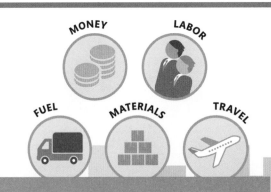

MONEY LABOR FUEL MATERIALS TRAVEL

BENEFITS OF SUSTAINABILITY

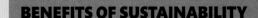

> **Increased loyalty** from donors, consumers, or service users who are willing to support an organization, product, or brand that aligns with their own values.

> **Managers who prioritize** the "triple bottom line"—CSR expert John Elkington's theory of social, environmental, and financial factors—can benefit the entire organization.

> **People working** for an ethical employer—such as UK retailer John Lewis, which treats employees "as partners"—are more effective due to working for a cause they believe in.

1 Assess the organization's impact on the local community, natural resources, and the resources used by suppliers.

2 Gain commitments from staff, suppliers, and stakeholders, then set targets and milestones.

✓ NEED TO KNOW

> **Corporate Social Responsibility (CSR)** provides independent certification for companies that meet standards of social and environmental performance.

> **United Nations Sustainable Development Goals** call for governments and organizations to achieve sustainability targets in 17 key areas—including equality, environmental degradation, and climate—by 2030.

81%
of global consumers believe that ethical shopping is essential

Cone Communications/Ebiquity Global CSR Study, 2015

3 Measure progress and report to stakeholders, then review plans and update as necessary.

4 Remain transparent and advertise the organization's philosophy, achievements, and goals.

ETHICAL STANDARDS

Placing ethical policy at the heart of an organization's strategy ensures that sustainability remains a business priority. Accreditations such as Fairtrade, Rainforest Alliance, and certified Organic—which ensure that goods and suppliers meet environmental and trading standards—bring financial benefits, since consumers are willing to pay higher prices for ethical products and services. For example, the UK market for organic vegetables increased by 5 percent in 2018, while nonorganic sales decreased. Likewise, sales of organic textiles, such as cotton, grew by 18 percent.

Managing Constraints

At the heart of the theory of constraints is the idea that a chain is no stronger than its weakest link. For managers, this means that their key task is to identify and manage the weakest parts of their organization.

Focus on limitations

The theory of constraints was developed by Israeli management guru Eliyahu Goldratt, first introduced in his book *The Goal* (1984). It is based on the principle that every company's most important task is to make a profit (which is true even of non-profit organizations). Goldratt views every organization as a system, or chain, of activities, whose success is controlled by three basic measures: inventory (money invested in the organization); operational expense (money used to turn inventory into sales); and throughput (the rate at which money is generated). Every system has at least one weak link, or constraint. If the constraint can be found and overcome (or controlled, if it is unavoidable), the organization is more likely to meet its goals. The key is to focus on the most significant limiting factor in an organization, since managing this constraint will produce the greatest benefit for the entire system. For example, keeping operational expenses low may make a department highly efficient, but it may not benefit the organization unless doing so also improves throughput.

Theory of constraints

Goldratt saw constraints (also known as bottlenecks) as the keys to productivity. By identifying and managing a constraint, a manager can significantly improve output. Conversely, by "fixing" an issue that is not a constraint, a manager could be allocating resources to the wrong area and making the situation worse.

Upstream

Throughput is normal here. Trying to fix the problem at this point may make things worse; for example, adding capacity may increase the buildup of work at the bottleneck.

"... the capacity of the plant is equal to the capacity of its bottlenecks."

Eliyahu Goldratt, *The Goal*, 1984

FIVE FOCUSING STEPS

Goldratt's five focusing steps are used to help an organization work around, or even with, its most significant constraints. The example below involves a company that manufactures washing machines but has lost business due to a high number of faults reported by customers.

IDENTIFY
Establish whether the constraint is internal or external, where it occurs in the system, and whether it involves resources, processes, staff, or policy.

EXPLOIT
Make the best improvements possible with the existing resources available; for example, focus resources on the parts that most likely need repair.

SUBORDINATE
Realign all the other parts of the system to fit around the constraint, for a smooth flow of activity. For example, build up a "buffer" of stock so that orders can be fulfilled.

ELEVATE
Mitigate or eliminate the constraint—for example, by repairing or replacing faulty machinery, or devising ways to make product repairs faster and easier.

DON'T STOP
Identify the next most significant constraint, and repeat steps 1 to 4 to minimize or eliminate it. Repeat the process for the lifetime of the business.

Bottleneck

This is the point at which the throughput, or flow of work, is restricted. Problems here reduce the efficiency of the whole process, but fixing these problems will solve the issue.

Downstream

Efficiency is reduced here since there isn't enough work coming through the system. However, making changes at this point (such as by adding capacity) will do nothing to solve the problem.

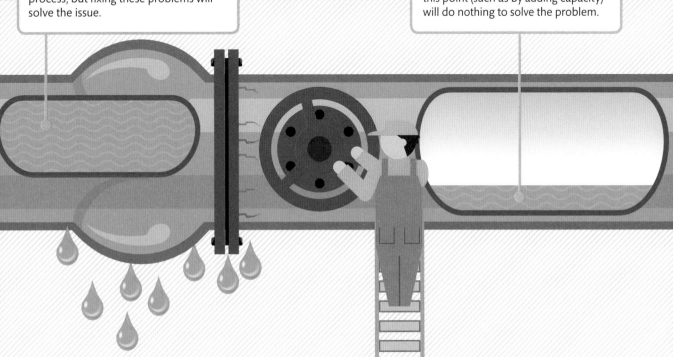

Business Cases

At some point, all managers are likely to have to write a business case to define the costs and benefits of a proposed course of action. This document is an essential tool that helps managers determine whether to invest in and proceed with a plan.

An essential overview

A business case summarizes the reasoning for starting a project or task. It is often presented in a well-structured written document. Writing a robust business case at the start of a project is a valuable exercise for managers to undertake; it helps consolidate ideas and plans, shape scope and direction, and identify gaps at an early stage.

Business cases are worth spending time on, since they provide essential information for those who need to make evidence-based, transparent decisions. For stakeholders, too, they explain the project's potential benefits. A business case also sets out a framework for implementing the project to focus actions and decisions on the stated goal, as well as to evaluate it.

The document typically includes the business opportunity, benefits, costs, risks, timescales, technical solutions, and resources required. In some sectors, such as local government, a business case may be even more comprehensive, as it is likely to be part of the formal decision-making process. The five case business model (see below) can be used in such instances.

The five case model

One best practice approach to preparing a business case is the five case model. This gives a comprehensive overview, looking beyond financial aspects to encompass wider considerations: the strategic case, commercial case, economic case, financial case, and management case. Setting out and exploring each aspect of the proposal enables the managers involved to make better-informed decisions and reduces the risk of wasting resources by exploring plans with a limited chance of success. Performing a cost-benefit analysis or calculating return on investment (see box, top right) are all part of putting together a sound business case. Producing a business case ensures that any projects that are implemented have the greatest chance of successfully achieving their goals.

STRATEGIC CASE

This demonstrates that the project will meet the organization's needs.

> **A good strategic fit** means that the project furthers the aims and objectives of the organization.

> **The SMART acronym** (see pp.148–149) can be used to sum up the project's goals.

> **A strong case for change** shows how the project meets the changing expectations or needs of the organization.

COMMERCIAL CASE

This shows that the project is commercially viable and what the deal will look like.

> **The deal should show value** for money and be well structured, with standards in place for the new services or project.

> **A suitable supplier** should be both available and able to meet the needs of the organization.

NEED TO KNOW

❯ **Return on investment (ROI)** measures gain or loss generated on an investment, relative to the amount of money invested.

❯ **Net present value (NPV)** calculates the future revenue that an investment will generate and discounts it to show what it is worth in today's money. It enables managers to make comparisons with alternative investment options.

❯ **Cost-benefit analysis (CBA)** compares the value of costs against benefits, which are assigned a monetary value.

"**A** sound business case **is a** foundation to effective **business decisions.**"

KPMG, multinational professional services network

ECONOMIC CASE

This indicates that the project will provide good value for money.

❯ **The best option** is selected after considering a range of options and is chosen for being the most cost-effective.

❯ **The best balance** of cost, benefit, and risk is considered and then decided on.

FINANCIAL CASE

The financial case shows that a project will be affordable.

❯ **Funding** shows how the project will be financed over a five-year period, including profit and loss and cash flow, and should indicate that the funding is both available and supported.

❯ **The projected costs** of moving to the new model or plan and delivering the new services are calculated and should be both realistic and affordable.

MANAGEMENT CASE

This sets out the plans for delivery, demonstrating that the project will be delivered effectively, that the organization has the capability to produce the project, and that the appropriate systems and processes are in place.

❯ **The inputs required** are listed and include the property, equipment and people needed, and the timescale for delivery.

❯ **Risks and technical considerations** are identified, as well as how to mitigate and resolve them, along with legal issues and the management of any assets.

Understanding Change

Organizations must be prepared to adapt if they are to keep up with a fast-changing business environment. However, change can be traumatic, and managers should be sensitive to how it affects their employees.

Turbulent times

In times of change, managers who hope for things to "get back to normal" fail to understand that change is the key to survival. Today, change is complex, multifaceted, and pervasive. Global business is evolving with technology, and the 21st-century workplace is being reshaped by connectivity, shifts in societal norms, and the blurring of boundaries between work and home life. Change management is designed to cope with this turbulence—it is a structured approach that ensures a smooth transformation and lasting benefits. Successful managers view change as a process, albeit a dynamic one, which occurs in response to internal and external

STATUS QUO

DISRUPTION

Shock
The first reaction to change is usually shock. This feeling may not last for long, but it is likely to affect an employee's performance.

Denial
After shock comes denial. The employee convinces themselves that the change will not affect them or that it may not even happen.

Anger
Once anger sets in, the employee will often look for someone within the organization to blame for the change.

Fear
As anger wears off, the employee is likely to realize that change is inevitable. They may feel isolated by their fear of the unknown.

The change curve

Psychiatrist Elisabeth Kübler-Ross's book *On Death and Dying* (1969) described the stages of grief, based on her work with terminally ill patients. This model is now used by organizations as a way of understanding how people deal with change and how their emotions may affect their performance. The "change curve" helps managers to communicate effectively and offer appropriate support. Kübler-Ross stressed that this is a long process and that people adjust in different ways.

factors. There are numerous change models that a manager can use (see below and pp.94–95), but the key focus must always be on how to encourage people to move from the present situation to the new one.

Successful change

Research shows that 70 percent of change management programs fail to achieve their goals. According to leading management consultants McKinsey, in the article "Changing Change Management" (2015), change fails largely due to employee resistance and a lack of executive support.

There are various ways in which managers can avoid these pitfalls. It is essential that they listen to their team members and convey information that is relevant to an individual's role. By considering what might happen in the future, managers can ensure that by the time change has been delivered, it will still be relevant. Strong leadership is also vital to success—those leading the change must be visible and unwavering in their support of staff members. By explaining why change is necessary and presenting it as a revolution, rather than evolution, leaders will help employees understand the process and embrace change.

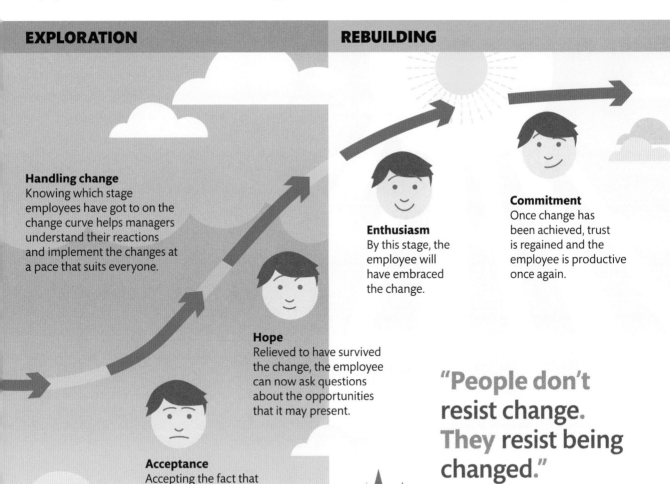

EXPLORATION

REBUILDING

Handling change
Knowing which stage employees have got to on the change curve helps managers understand their reactions and implement the changes at a pace that suits everyone.

Enthusiasm
By this stage, the employee will have embraced the change.

Commitment
Once change has been achieved, trust is regained and the employee is productive once again.

Hope
Relieved to have survived the change, the employee can now ask questions about the opportunities that it may present.

Acceptance
Accepting the fact that things are changing will help the employee banish gloom and begin to feel optimistic.

"People don't resist change. They resist being changed."

Peter Senge, US scientist and author

Change Models

Over time, change management theorists have introduced various models to guide organizations through the complex and dynamic process of change, taking into account the emotional responses of employees.

Putting people first

The earliest change management models were influenced by studies of how people dealt with loss and life changes (see pp.92–93). These studies emphasized that people react differently to change, and so change management models must take employees' varying emotional needs into account. In 1962, sociologist Everett Rogers was the first to talk about how people take different periods of time to adapt to new ideas, introducing the concept of "early adopters"— people who are quick to embrace a new technology, company, product, or way of working. Early adopters tend to play an active role in the change management process.

Kurt Lewin's three-stage change model (see box, right) has been popular since the 1950s and remains valid today. Management consultants McKinsey developed their own 7-S model (see pp.96–97) in the 1980s, which outlines seven essential elements in managing change and takes account of the effects of change on employees. John Kotter's eight-step model, from his 1996 book *Leading Change*, is one of the most popular models for integrating required new behaviors into successful organizational change (see below).

"If you want truly to understand something, try to change it."

Kurt Lewin

One step at a time

Change management expert John Kotter came up with eight steps for leading a successful change process. He stressed the importance of involving employees in the process at every stage, preparing them for change before implementing it.

1

Create urgency
Talk about what is happening. If the whole team understands that change is needed urgently, it will progress more smoothly.

2

Form a powerful coalition
Convince team members to embrace change by being a strong leader with visible allies.

3

Create a vision
Develop a clear vision for change so that the team can see how the future will be different from the present.

4

Communicate the vision
Convey the vision powerfully and as often as possible, using a range of communication channels.

LEWIN'S CHANGE MODEL

Psychologist Kurt Lewin outlined a three-stage model for change that influenced many later models. He emphasized that employees must first recognize the need for change. Then, once the change is implemented and fully integrated, the new way is accepted and becomes the norm.

Unfreeze
Build awareness of why change is necessary to avoid resistance from employees.

Change
Set goals and communicate with the team, involving them in the change process.

Refreeze
Embed the change into team culture and celebrate the new status quo.

5

Empower action
Begin to build the structure for change, offering support to reluctant staff and rewarding those who help.

6

Create quick wins
Aim for a series of small short-term wins rather than one big long-term target. Success will motivate a team.

7

Build on the change
Always look for improvements. Each small win is a chance to identify what has gone well and what has not.

8

Make it stick
For lasting success, embed the vision in the organization's everyday values and encourage all employees to embrace it.

NUDGE THEORY

The book *Nudge Theory* (2008) by R. Thaler and C. Sunstein, explains the idea of encouraging, or "nudging," change rather than trying to impose it in a traditional way. People are less likely to resist change when they have an element of control. The UK government set up a nudge unit to address policy and service issues. Late payment of taxes was an ongoing problem, but officials found that adding a note to the late payment letter—saying that most people pay their taxes on time—increased tax payment rates significantly.

The 7-S Model

The 7-S model is considered the definitive strategic planning tool. It helps managers understand and assess the key elements of their organization that influence its ability to change.

Interdependent elements

The 7-S model was developed in *In Search of Excellence* (1982) by Tom Peters and Robert Waterman at management consultancy McKinsey & Company. Until then, management theory had focused on the use of resources and business structure. However, as organizations grew larger and more complex, coordination began to be seen as equally important.

The 7-S model introduced the idea that seven aspects of an organization need to be aligned in order for it to achieve its objectives. These elements are divided into "hard" and "soft" groups. The hard elements are strategy, structure, and systems, which are usually associated with management and leadership and tend to involve measurable goals and physical tasks. The soft elements are staff, skills, style, and shared values.

These are just as important as the hard elements, because they establish the culture and environment that enable teams to achieve their goals. The seven aspects are equally important. They are also interdependent so that a change to one element has to be coordinated with all the others.

Using the 7-S model

The first step is to analyze the elements to see how well they are aligned with each other; there are numerous online checklists, with questions about each element, to help with this process. Next, the ideal alignment of elements for the organization should be determined. Then the desired improvement or change should be defined and implemented.

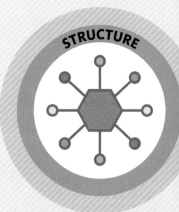

The hierarchies that determine who is accountable to whom, and the communication lines between them.

 NEED TO KNOW

❯ **Shared values** lie at the core of the 7-S model. They raise the first question of strategic analysis: does the plan accord with the organization's values?

❯ **The 7-S model** is particularly useful in times of change, such as during mergers, acquisitions, reorganizations, or the introduction of new systems.

The capabilities of the staff, both individually and collectively.

All the members of the organization, from its interns to its CEO.

Planning for change

The 7-S model is most often used to identify performance problems and to highlight any discrepancies between the present situation and the desired goal. This enables managers to specify areas that can be improved, predict the likely effects of any changes, implement new strategies, and plan for any disruptions. It is particularly useful during mergers, when questions of purpose and value come to the fore.

ADAPTING THE MODEL

The 7-S model has been criticized for focusing only on internal activities and giving relatively little attention to important activities outside the organization. In response, two other Ss may be added: Stakeholders and Setting (context). With increasing concerns today about the global environment, a further S is being added: Sustainability.

STRATEGY

The overarching plan for achieving goals and gaining advantage over competition.

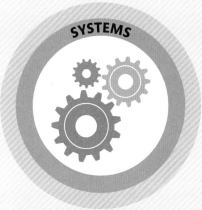

SYSTEMS

All the activities and procedures that staff members use to perform their jobs.

HARD ELEMENTS

These are the elements traditionally associated with running an organization. They are relatively easy to define and influence compared to the soft elements.

SOFT ELEMENTS

These elements shape the culture of an organization rather than the day-to-day tasks. They establish the purpose and focus of the organization and its people.

STYLE

The manner in which managers interact with their teams.

SHARED VALUES

The organization's mission and core values. These set the vision and ethical standards for all employees.

"A company doesn't run if its people don't run with it."

Ping Fu, US Vice President of 3D Systems, 2016

Data and Information

To make effective and timely decisions, managers must often first process data to find the information they need. In an era of extreme data gathering, this requires a modern data-management strategy.

Effective management

Managers' decisions must be informed by facts, so they need easy access to relevant, accurate data on any given issue and a reliable way to analyze it and glean the information they require. Today, this can present a real challenge because companies often hold a large volume of data relating to customers, financial transactions, marketing campaigns, service inquiries,

and much more. Such a wealth of data can potentially enable enterprises to operate more efficiently and capitalize on new business opportunities. To do so, however, requires an appropriate data-management strategy. The best models provide easy access to essential company data and sift through emails and social media streams for facts, figures, or observations (raw data) that may be of use to the organization.

Gathering data

Internal and external data may be input into the system by employees or collected electronically from different sources.

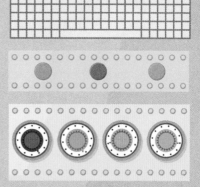

Receiving data

Data analysts, assisted by computer algorithms (a type of artificial intelligence) help sift and store incoming data in relevant areas. A system that links all types of data is the most useful because it allows different data sets to be compared.

Handling data

Managers who have to process data on a variety of topics in order to make decisions need the data to be relevant, accurate, and up to date and the retrieval process to be speedy and efficient. Fully integrated data-management systems make the process easier, enabling managers to check the source of a set of statistics, for example, or compare similar data.

DATA, INFORMATION, KNOWLEDGE, WISDOM

Often illustrated as a pyramid, the "DIKW model" describes how information stems from data, knowledge from information, and wisdom from knowledge. This linear process of analyzing and understanding data helps managers make good decisions.

Data is made up of a jumble of facts, symbols, measurements, numbers, or observations. Without a context, it is meaningless; it needs to be organized, interpreted, and verified by a person or computer in order to become meaningful—to become information. Major managerial decisions, such as whether to make people redundant, are based on the information gleaned from data.

Making the right decision also requires knowledge, however, which comes when information has been received and properly understood. Knowledge enables a manager to see patterns in information and make predictions. Their own wisdom then allows them to use this knowledge to best effect.

✓ NEED TO KNOW

❯ **Enterprise Data Management (EDM)** concerns defining, integrating, retrieving, and managing data.

❯ **General Data Protection Regulation (GDPR)** is a European law governing the use of any data from which a person can be identified.

❯ **Structured data**, such as names or dates, is easily classified; unstructured data, such as emails, is more difficult to analyze.

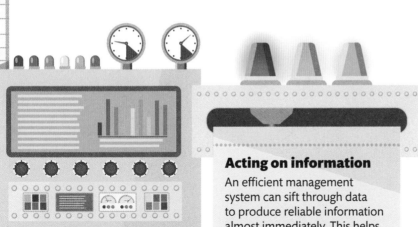

Reviewing data

Ideally, the data in a data-management system will be organized in such a way that managers can retrieve what they need quickly, check that data is current and accurate, and compare it with other data in order to turn it into information.

Acting on information

An efficient management system can sift through data to produce reliable information almost immediately. This helps managers make decisions and react more quickly—for instance, to changing customer preferences—giving a company a competitive edge. In most cases, however, a manager's experience in analyzing data remains invaluable.

1.7
the number of megabytes each person is estimated to produce every second

Data Never Sleeps 6.0, Domo, 2017

Decision-making

The ability to make balanced decisions, even when information is incomplete, is indispensable in a manager. Clear decision-making instills confidence in the team and ensures progress toward goals.

Analysis or intuition?

Making a decision involves defining the objective to be achieved, gathering the necessary information, assessing possible solutions, and then making a firm choice. To aid effective decision-making, managers need the complementary skills of rational analysis and intuition. Step-by-step analysis can help when there is time available and a more considered decision is required. However, the pace of business in many organizations often requires managers to make quick decisions with limited information; in such situations, intuition can be valuable. Many managers may have a preferred decision-making style. Some managers insist on detail and analysis—others think that this can derail decisions, so they rely on intuition honed by experience. The best managers draw on their preferred style and work to develop alternatives.

MAKING SWIFT DECISIONS

According to Danish organization theorists Kristian Kreiner and Søren Christensen, managers should make decisions quickly, even with minimal information. Their model shows that the consequences of a manager's decision relate inversely to the extent of knowledge available: the less knowledge, the greater the consequences, and vice versa. Although a manager may initially want more information on an issue, it will have a decreasing impact on the final decision made.

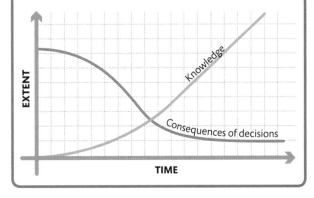

Mapping a decision

When making a complex decision, it is important to evaluate all the possible consequences—intended and unintended—first. One way of doing this is by creating a "yes/no" chart or diagram. Managers can use this to map out their thoughts and to explain their decision to those affected by it.

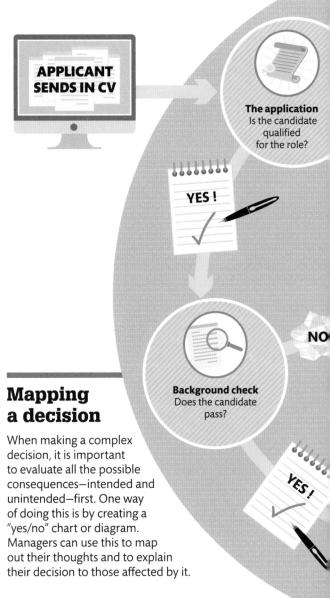

APPLICANT SENDS IN CV

The application
Is the candidate qualified for the role?

YES !

Background check
Does the candidate pass?

NO

YES !

"**Stay** committed
to your decisions,
but stay flexible
in your approach."

Tony Robbins, life coach, 2012

Expectations
Will the role meet
the candidate's
needs?

YES !

**OFFER
THEM
THE
JOB**

NO

YES !

NO

**REJECT
APPLICATION**

NO

Personality
Would the candidate
fit in with the team's
culture?

NO

YES !

At interview
Does the candidate show
ability, understanding,
and experience?

SEVEN KEY STEPS

To help make clear, effective decisions,
there are seven essential steps that
managers should follow:

1. Identify the decision that needs
to be made. Define the main issue
and the desired outcome.

2. Collect relevant information.
Seek advice from others who may
have knowledge of the issue.

3. Determine all viable options.
Make a list of at least four, to give
a broad range of possible solutions.

4. Assess each option. Establish the
pros and cons; evaluate each option
for feasibility and desirability.

5. Choose the option or combination
of options most likely to succeed and
with the most acceptable risk level.

6. Take action, identify the resources
necessary—including staff—and make
a plan to implement the decision.

7. Review the decision regularly to
ensure that it is still the most effective
course of action.

Force-field Analysis

A successful organization is one that is constantly evolving. Force-field analysis is a tool for managing change. It helps managers to identify the forces that encourage change and those that work against it.

Positive forces

The principles of Force-field analysis were developed in the 1940s by social psychologist Kurt Lewin and described in *Field Theory in Social Science* (1951). The basis of Lewin's idea is that in every organization there are positive forces that drive change, and restraining forces that produce resistance to change. Where there is equilibrium between the forces, there is stability and little change—but when restraining forces are outstripped by positive (driving) forces, change becomes possible. In order for change to occur, either the positive forces need to be increased or the restraining forces must be weakened.

Both types of forces may come from inside or outside an organization. Positive external forces might include increased customer demand or the emergence of new

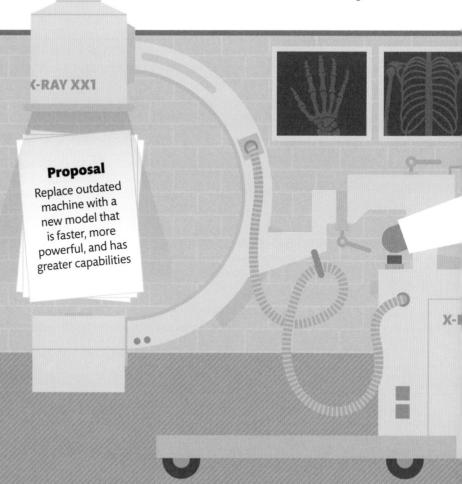

Upgrading medical equipment

A hospital manager has a situation in which an item of medical equipment has become outdated and may need to be upgraded. However, this is far from straightforward, not least because of the staff training required and disruption during installation. The manager works with the team to produce a Force-field analysis to show all the forces that need to be considered. On scoring the forces from 1 to 5, the team can see that the driving forces outweigh the restraining forces and so they buy into the required change.

Proposal
Replace outdated machine with a new model that is faster, more powerful, and has greater capabilities

X-RAY XX1

technology; internal forces might include a need to increase the organization's profits, to update equipment, or to change personnel.

Restraining external forces might include a tough market or stringent regulations; internal forces might be factors such as increased costs and disruption to workflow.

Managing change

Employee resistance to change can be one major internal restraint. A manager can minimize this resistance by first discussing any changes with their team. Drawing up a Force-field analysis diagram together with the team can provide a good visual summary. The manager defines the specific goal of the change they want to see. The team then identifies both the driving forces and restraining forces. They evaluate and rate each of the forces—from 1 (weak) to 5 (strong)—and figure out totals for each side. The team also determines which of these forces can be influenced or have some flexibility for change. The manager then, possibly with the team, develops a strategy for how to strengthen driving forces and weaken restraining ones. Finally, the manager will prioritize action steps, identifying resources needed to implement them.

The benefits of a Force-field analysis are that it allows time for a manager and team to discuss issues in depth, voice concerns, and offer solutions in order to reach consensus. Potential pitfalls are the subjective nature of the scoring, division in the team between those for and against change, and an incomplete picture if not all take team members participate.

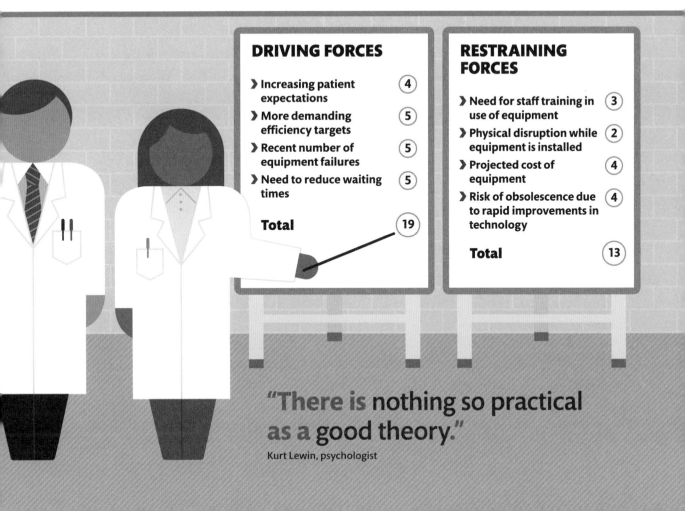

DRIVING FORCES

> **Increasing patient expectations** (4)
> **More demanding efficiency targets** (5)
> **Recent number of equipment failures** (5)
> **Need to reduce waiting times** (5)

Total (19)

RESTRAINING FORCES

> **Need for staff training in use of equipment** (3)
> **Physical disruption while equipment is installed** (2)
> **Projected cost of equipment** (4)
> **Risk of obsolescence due to rapid improvements in technology** (4)

Total (13)

"There is nothing so practical as a good theory."
Kurt Lewin, psychologist

SWOT Analysis

SWOT analysis is a simple but powerful tool that managers can use to identify internal and external factors likely to affect an organization's performance, across every sector of its operations.

Surveying the landscape

Developed by US management consultant Albert S. Humphrey in 1966 using data from Fortune 500 companies, SWOT analysis is a systematic, creative tool for managers that examines the Strengths, Weaknesses, Opportunities, and Threats that an organization may encounter. It can be used for day-to-day business operations, one-off projects, or developing new business strategies. It could also be used to examine long-term market opportunities or to engage personnel in formulating an organization's strategy.

A manager using SWOT analysis would begin by identifying internal strengths and weaknesses. These are factors that lie within the control of the manager or organization and so might include staff, product portfolio, marketing expertise, manufacturing capability, and organizational structure. Next, the manager evaluates external opportunities and threats. These are factors beyond the organization's control and so might include changing customer habits, environmental sustainability, the economic outlook, or technological advances—including social media marketing and internet selling tools.

Setting clear business objectives, such as operational or financial goals, is also central to a SWOT analysis. When managers have identified internal and external factors, they can assess their positive or negative impact on achieving business objectives.

PEST ANALYSIS

PEST analysis, thought to have originated with Harvard professor Francis Aguilar, is an acronym for Political, Economic, Sociological, and Technological. The acronym, which appears in various forms (see pp.72–73), can help managers identify external factors that might influence an organization. A PEST analysis should be conducted prior to undertaking a SWOT analysis.

Taking stock

SWOT analyses are useful when making key decisions, such as expanding a business. Freda Flour manages a bakery on the north side of town, specializing in artisan bread and gluten-free cakes. It is very successful, with a loyal customer base. Freda wants to open a second branch on the south side of town but knows another bakery is already established there. She does a SWOT analysis to evaluate potential risks and rewards.

"It is not the manager's job to prevent risks. It is the manager's job to make it safe to take them."

Ed Catmull, cofounder of Pixar Animation Studios, 2014

STRENGTHS

> **High-quality** ingredients
> **Differentiated** products
> **Loyal customer base** at the existing bakery
> **Specialist baking** knowledge

WEAKNESSES

> **High retail price** due to artisanal methods and ingredient costs
> **Premium products** limit market
> **Only one staff member**, Fred, has specialist baking knowledge

SWOT BLUEPRINT

SWOT analysis works best with open questions. For example, a manager might ask:

> **Strengths:** What do customers love about our products? What do we do better than other companies in the area?
> **Weaknesses:** What could we do better? Why do customers not like our products /buy from us?
> **Opportunities:** What changes in trends or weaknesses in our competitors can we exploit?
> **Threats:** What could our competitors do that would affect us? What social/shopping trends might threaten us?

OPPORTUNITIES

> **Growing trend** in healthy eating
> **Organic grocery** adjoining new site complements bakery
> **Heavy traffic** due to new site's location near train station

THREATS

> **Potential price increases** of artisan flour
> **Existing bakery** charges less due to not selling a premium product
> **Supermarket** offers online delivery of gluten-free and artisan products

STRATEGIC PLANNING

After addressing each finding from the SWOT analysis, Freda makes the following plans:

> **Strengths:** Develop strong relationships with customers at new shop to replicate existing loyal customer base
> **Weaknesses:** Recruit and train specialist baker for new shop
> **Opportunities:** Cater to growing interest in healthy eating by sourcing ethically produced ingredients
> **Threats:** Source cheaper ingredients or cut profit

Critical Path Analysis

Critical path analysis is a project-management tool for scheduling activities. Prioritizing and plotting tasks along a path gives a clear overview of the whole project and allows resources to be planned and optimized.

Optimizing project work

Critical path analysis enables a manager to schedule the tasks required to complete a project in the correct sequence and in the most time-efficient way. It also helps avoid conflicting priorities and bottlenecks. The first step is to identify tasks that are "critical," upon which others depend, and to plot them in the correct order, creating the "critical path." The manager should then estimate the time required to complete each task, which when added together gives the total time necessary for the project. Noncritical, or "floating," tasks are plotted parallel to the main path at appropriate stages in the project, and are completed within the overall time frame.

Building a house

Critical path analysis is a term that was coined by James Kelly and Morgan Walker in 1956 while developing the Manhattan Project. The model is ideal for planning complex projects that involve precise scheduling of multiple human and material resources, such as constructing a house. The simplified plan shown here highlights 11 key activities on a critical path of 34 days—the maximum time to complete this project. Identifying dependencies—activities that are reliant on other tasks—determines the scheduling and reveals where a delay in a single activity risks the whole project being delayed.

✓ **NEED TO KNOW**

> **Fast tracking** is the process of undertaking multiple floating activities in parallel to reduce the overall project time.

> **Crashing** is when additional resources are allocated to a task to complete it more quickly.

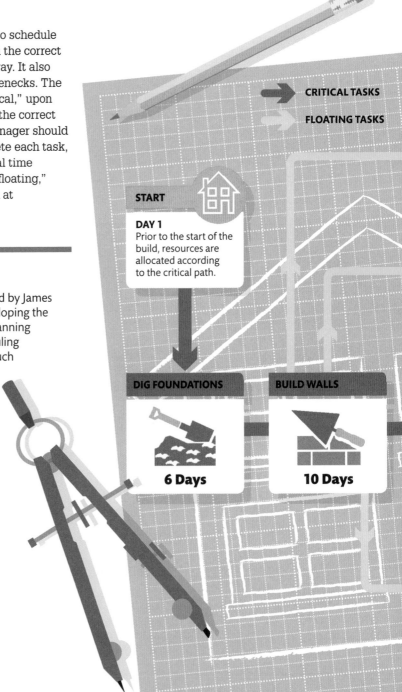

CRITICAL TASKS

FLOATING TASKS

START

DAY 1
Prior to the start of the build, resources are allocated according to the critical path.

DIG FOUNDATIONS

6 Days

BUILD WALLS

10 Days

"How does a project get to be a year late? One day at a time."

Frederick Brooks, US computer scientist, 1975

PROS AND CONS

❯ **Pro** Enables detailed assessment of requirements of each activity

❯ **Pro** Allows optimal allocation of resources

❯ **Pro** Can reduce risks and costs

❯ **Con** Only as reliable as the assumptions and estimates made

❯ **Con** No guarantee of success—every task still needs to be efficiently managed

❯ **Con** Identifying spare time does not make resources available

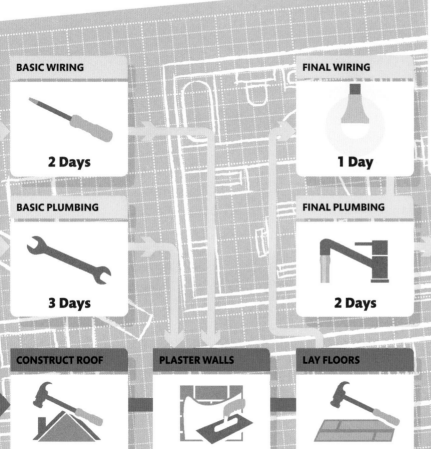

BASIC WIRING

2 Days

FINAL WIRING

1 Day

BASIC PLUMBING

3 Days

FINAL PLUMBING

2 Days

DECORATE

3 Days

CONSTRUCT ROOF

5 Days

PLASTER WALLS

10 Days

LAY FLOORS

3 Days

GARDEN AND LANDSCAPING

3 Days

END

DAY 34
If labor and materials are allotted to each task as scheduled, the build will take 34 days.

Problem-solving

Dealing with the many problems that occur within an organization is part of a manager's remit. The goal is to understand what went wrong and generate solutions that help to prevent a recurrence.

Opportunity for learning

While a key goal of management is to prevent problems, detecting, analyzing, and solving them effectively when they do occur is equally important (see pp.110–111). Varied issues, from nondelivery of raw materials to a security alert or a harassment claim, demand both workable solutions and measures to stop them from happening again.

Handled correctly, problems can be opportunities for learning and improvement. Skillful managers develop the ability to think through a problem systematically. They must assess its priority, uncover the facts, pinpoint its root cause, and work toward the best solution. Mastering this process, which can be applied to most problems, helps to avoid further complications. Managers who can handle problems effectively are key to an organization's success.

The plan of action

The problems that managers are likely to face range from minor issues to full-blown crises. The task of problem solving demands the ability to sift through facts, asking the right questions, to diagnose precisely what has gone wrong. The step-by-step approach shown here is designed to reach a solution, via analysis and discussion, that can be accepted by all. Achieving that goal consistently when problems arise strengthens teams and contributes to the health of an organization.

1 Understand the problem

Pinpoint and prioritize the issue:

> **Identify** its nature and how critical it is—whether there will be significant consequences if it is not resolved.

> **Rate** its urgency and whether waiting will make the problem worse.

> **Consider** what can be done and whether a makeshift solution might prevent things from getting worse.

3 Generate a solution

Only when the real problem is understood should a manager start to explore ways to solve it. For example:

> **Involve** others to get different perspectives.

> **Break down** big issues into small, bite-size, solvable problems.

> **Think laterally** to find a creative and indirect approach.

> "Problems are only opportunities in work clothes."

Henry Kaiser, US industrialist, 1967

2 Identify all elements

Look at the problem from multiple perspectives:

> **Take** time and listen to all those who are involved.

> **Identify** the root cause (see pp. 78–79)—address this rather than symptoms.

> **Avoid** assumptions and establish facts.

> **Ask** the right questions (see box, below right).

4 Act on a plan

Settle the issue, following these steps:

> **Select** the best solution.

> **Write** it down, summarizing any recommendations.

> **Communicate** and enact the solution with all those involved.

> **Find** ways to prevent the problem from recurring, if possible.

ASK THE RIGHT QUESTIONS

Effective problem-solving involves suspending judgment and asking the right questions. The best questions are open-ended and start with words that Rudyard Kipling called his "six honest serving-men": who, what, when, where, why, and how. Focusing and enlarging on these questions will help avoid generalizations and establish accurate facts.

WHO? **WHAT?** **WHEN?** **WHERE?** **WHY?** **HOW?**

Identifying Causes

Problem-solving is a key part of a manager's role, but not all problems have obvious solutions. In order to understand—and hopefully fix—a problem, a manager must first identify and analyze all of its possible causes.

Digging to the roots

Developed by Japanese organizational theorist Kaoru Ishikawa in the 1960s, Cause and Effect Analysis enables managers to define problems clearly, solve them, and ensure that they never recur.

The starting point is to define the problem: what is happening, where is it happening, and who is affected by it. The next stage is to group all the possible causes into six categories: processes, equipment, materials, people, environment, and management. The best way to do this is to draw a "fishbone diagram" (see below). This depicts the six categories as vertical lines projecting from the central "spine" of the problem. From each of these lines, the manager then draws a series of horizontal lines on which they identify all the problem's possible causes—a process that may involve detailed investigation, such as interviewing staff at all levels.

When all the possibilities have been identified, it should be clear to the manager where the problem lies and what action should be taken to solve it. This action should be taken swiftly and details of the lessons learned made known throughout the organization.

Fishbone diagram

In this example of a fishbone diagram, a production process for a component has been generating too many rejects, and thus a high level of waste. The problem is defined at the head of the "fish" and is then broken down into Ishikawa's six categories. Each cause is divided further into subcauses; for example, the "people" cause includes factors such as lack of training and conflict within the team. The final step is the analysis of the diagram. In this example, the main cause of the problem is identified as the use of substandard material.

PROBLEM: 20% WASTE

Cause 1: Processes

- ❯ Process speed unreliable
- ❯ Drying temperature too high
- ❯ Insufficient time between stages

- ❯ Machine running too fast
- ❯ Cannot control drying temperature
- ❯ Machine breaks down with no warning

Cause 2: Equipment

"Failure is the seed of success."

Kaoru Ishikawa

THE "FIVE WHYS" TECHNIQUE

A quick way of getting to the heart of a problem is by using the "five whys" technique pioneered by Toyota. This involves repeatedly asking "Why?" in order to trace the cause of a problem. A manager can usually do this in five stages, the answer to the first question becoming the basis of the second question, and so on. For example, if a factory worker falls and is injured, the following five questions can get to the root of the problem.

A FACTORY WORKER FALLS, PROMPTING FIVE QUESTIONS ABOUT THE CAUSE

❯ **1. Why?** There was an oil spill on the floor in the machining department.

❯ **2. Why?** One of the pressing machines was leaking oil.

❯ **3. Why?** The seal was of poor quality.

❯ **4. Why?** Low-cost seals, below standard specification, had been purchased from a new supplier.

❯ **5. Why?** A company-wide directive had been issued for teams to cut manufacturing costs.

Cause 3: Materials

❯ Inconsistent quality in raw materials

❯ Lower-grade material purchased

❯ Subparts not assembled correctly

Cause 5: Environment

❯ Insufficient space around machine

❯ Poor ventilation causes overheating

❯ Untidy work area obscures source of problem

 NEED TO KNOW

❯ **Solvable causes** are the parts of a problem that can be solved—that is the area the manager should seek to address.

❯ **Insolvable causes** are those parts of a problem that cannot be solved. These must be identified so that the manager does not waste time trying to fix them.

❯ **Cause screening** is a method of evaluating the potential impact of a cause and how easy it is to prevent that cause.

❯ Conflict in team

❯ Lack of formal training

❯ Team feels unable to raise issues with manager

❯ Manager unskilled at handling change

❯ No clear chain of responsibility

❯ Targets based on quantity rather than quality

Cause 4: People

Cause 6: Management

Design Thinking

Originally developed to identify customers' needs, design thinking is an approach that all managers can adopt in order to pinpoint and resolve complex and challenging problems within their organization.

Solving problems

While many of the problems a manager encounters are clear-cut, such as a damaged machine or a lack of funds, others are less defined—for example, why staff are underperforming. In these situations, design thinking is a useful tool for finding solutions. Unlike the traditional approach to problem-solving (see pp. 108–109), which involves identifying the root cause, this method focuses the manager's attention on those who will benefit from the solution, such as staff.

Design thinking is a step-by-step technique by which a manager should seek to understand and solve the problem from the perspective of those involved. The first steps are to understand who those people are and to establish their needs—for example, the roles of the staff and the tools they need in order to perform better. From this information, the manager should then think laterally and creatively, involving those in question, to find ideas. The next steps are to develop potential solutions, such as new working practices or new management structures, and to test them out before implementing them. Although time-consuming, design thinking enables managers to develop bespoke solutions that benefit specific staff—and thus the organization as a whole.

Case study: Apple Inc.

Cofounded by Steve Jobs in 1976, Apple Inc. began to struggle in the 1980s and '90s due to intense competition in the computer market. Jobs, who had left Apple, returned in 1997 and used design thinking to develop products based on what customers actually wanted. Apple launched the iMac in 1998 and the iPhone in 2007—both huge successes. The process Jobs followed can be used by any manager, whether developing new products or seeking to solve tricky problems.

1

2

Define
Based on all the information gathered from those involved, define the problem to be solved. Focus on their needs, not the organization's.

Empathize
Engage with people and research their needs. Fully understand what they actually require before trying to meet their needs.

PHONE

PRESENT

SIX THINKING HATS

Edward de Bono, a leading authority on thinking skills and author of *Six Thinking Hats* (1985), developed the idea of six approaches in which differently coloured hats each represent a different style of thinking.

In order to solve problems effectively, managers should experiment by "wearing" different hats – thinking in different ways – and should also encourage others in their team to do the same. team to do the same.

NEUTRALITY	**OPTIMISM**	**JUDGMENT**	**EMOTION**	**CREATIVITY**	**ORGANIZING**
Focus on facts and data only to establish all the relevant information.	Explore the positive aspects and benefits of ideas and plans.	Consider the pitfalls and dangers and possible consequences.	Assess your gut reactions and instincts. Seek and express opinions.	Consider all possibilities, alternatives, and fresh ideas.	Define the issue, manage the thinking process, and summarize.

Ideate
Brainstorm ideas to solve the problem. This requires creativity, analytic judgment, and a willingness to take risks.

4

Prototype
Once ideas have been generated, develop them into workable solutions or prototype products. These should be simple and user-friendly and solve the problem identified at Stage 2.

5

Test
Test the solutions or new products on those who will use them, so their strengths and weaknesses can be assessed. Testing may show that the problem needs to be redefined.

HELLO?

"Most people make the mistake of thinking design is what it looks like. Design is how it works."

Steve Jobs, cofounder of Apple Inc., 2003

FUTURE

Resolving Deadlocks

When different parties cannot agree on an issue, a manager may need to step in. A strategy that dissects the problem can break a deadlock and help the parties find a mutually acceptable solution.

Breaking a vicious cycle

A deadlock can occur when two or more parties have different solutions to a problem and refuse to change their demands. Whatever the reason for such an impasse—whether a business deal, an internal organizational matter, or a negotiation with a third party—considerable diplomacy is required. A manager may need to act as a mediator if the deadlock involves department members or the department itself is in dispute with another sector of the organization or an outside body. Typically, each party believes it has the correct solution and that the other party is wrong.

A vicious cycle can then begin, in which each party is more concerned with saving face than reexamining the original issue. It becomes a battle that neither side wants to be seen to lose.

A manager has to step back from the dispute and view the arguments of each party fairly and impartially. In an internal deadlock, it may be advisable to call in a neutral individual to act as a mediator. Adopting a strategy that identifies each viewpoint, areas in which parties disagree and why, as well as points on which they all concur, can help produce a compromise that breaks the deadlock.

Group decision

A company makes organic T-shirts in the US. Manager Mary has two senior team members—George and Mark—who are in deadlock over the introduction of new machines. Each has different assumptions, interests, and information due to their different roles. George is head of finance and is worried about the capital cost because he is responsible for profitability. Mark is head of human resources and worries about the training time required and whether further organizational change will affect motivation. Mary needs to get agreement from the team and convenes a meeting, following a five-step process. By sharing information, they agree that the new machines are worth the investment.

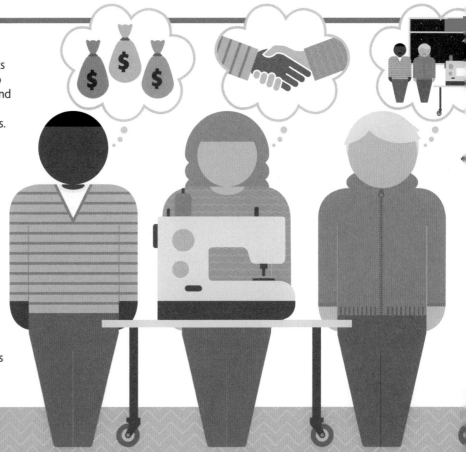

CONNECTING THE DOTS

Organizational psychologist Roger Schwarz describes deadlocks as an adult version of a connect-the-dots puzzle. In a team deadlock, the dots represent the assumptions, interests, and information that each person uses to create their own picture. The line connecting the dots is the reasoning process, but each team member has their own set of dots and connects those dots in different ways to arrive at what they believe is the correct solution. Arguing about competing solutions without understanding the assumptions, interests, and information that generated that picture in the first place merely maintains the deadlock.

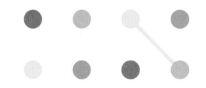

"... deadlocks ... have at least this advantage ... they force us to think."

Jawaharlal Nehru, first
Prime Minister of India, 1942

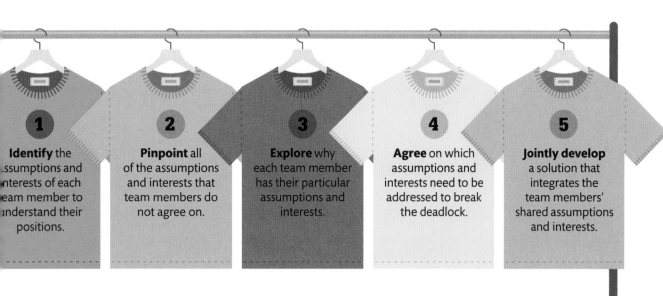

1 **Identify** the assumptions and interests of each team member to understand their positions.

2 **Pinpoint** all of the assumptions and interests that team members do not agree on.

3 **Explore** why each team member has their particular assumptions and interests.

4 **Agree** on which assumptions and interests need to be addressed to break the deadlock.

5 **Jointly develop** a solution that integrates the team members' shared assumptions and interests.

Business Processes

Like a project, a process is a series of linked activities. But while a project is temporary and delivers change—or a new product or service—a process is part of the organization's routine workflow.

A series of steps

The concept of a business process originated in manufacturing, where materials are transformed from their raw state through a series of steps into a final finished product. But processes occur elsewhere, too. In the case of a restaurant, the process may involve receiving a reservation, greeting the customer, taking their order, and preparing and serving the food.

It is widely believed that businesses can be run with four high level operating processes. These are win the order; supply the order; service the customer; and develop new products or services. Each of these operating processes can be broken down into smaller steps. For example, the process of winning an order can be subdivided into: attracting customers (via marketing activities) and closing the order (via sales

Process mapping

Managers can analyse business processes to see whether the steps involved are adding value by being necessary, efficient, and effective. Flowcharts are used to help understand stages of a process—in this example, reserving a table in a restaurant. The next step is to design and implement an improved process. The improvements may include removing unnecessary steps or finding better ways of doing things, such as introducing automation.

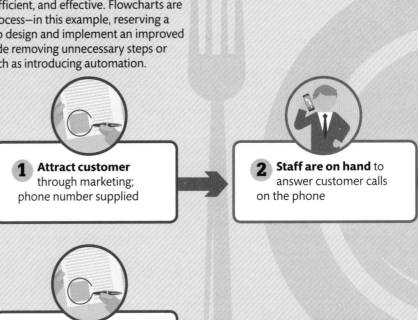

EXISTING PROCESS
This is a restaurant's current reservation process. The employees need to be available to answer the phone and to look through the calendar to find suitable dates for the customer, requiring a series of steps.

1 Attract customer through marketing; phone number supplied

2 Staff are on hand to answer customer calls on the phone

IMPROVED PROCESS
This is the desired situation in the organization and it is set alongside the existing situation for direct comparison. In this scenario, the series of steps involved in reserving and selecting dates is streamlined into one step.

1 Attract customer through marketing; website supplied

activities). Managers must aim to understand and improve any process—and its associated steps —under their care. Process mapping (see below) was designed for this.

Two kinds of processes

Processes are often described as either "value adding" or "nonvalue adding" (see pp.118–119). The former are part of operating processes that offer the customer or user values. The latter are support processes, such as IT or accounts, which do not provide direct value to the user or customer.

SWIM LANES

The actions in a process map (see below) can be organized into "swim lanes" to make it clearer who is performing each action. For instance, a customer complaint might prompt an organization to try to resolve the issue, and these activities can be tracked across departments or to external contractors.

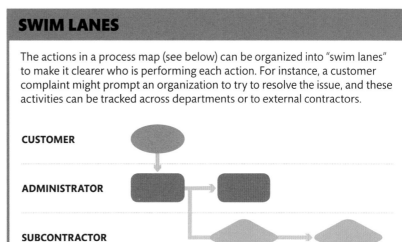

CUSTOMER

ADMINISTRATOR

SUBCONTRACTOR

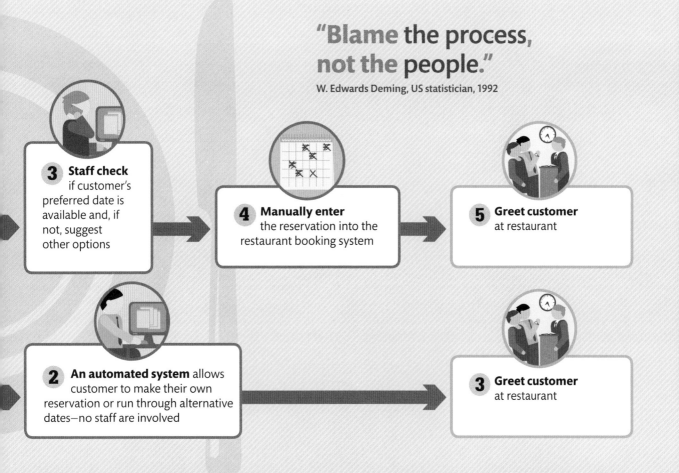

"Blame the process, not the people."

W. Edwards Deming, US statistician, 1992

3 **Staff check** if customer's preferred date is available and, if not, suggest other options

4 **Manually enter** the reservation into the restaurant booking system

5 **Greet customer** at restaurant

2 **An automated system** allows customer to make their own reservation or run through alternative dates—no staff are involved

3 **Greet customer** at restaurant

Value Chain

A value chain is a set of activities through which goods or services are developed. Managers need to ensure that each activity is working efficiently in order to maximize the value of the end product.

Value chain management

The concept of the "value chain" was introduced by US academic Michael Porter in his 1985 book *Competitive Advantage: Creating and Sustaining Superior Performance*. A value chain comprises all the activities, from the input of raw materials to distribution, that add value to the end product. For an organization to make a profit, the final value of a product or service must exceed the cost of creating it.

Value-chain analysis involves breaking down an operation into smaller parts so that it is easy to see what is happening at each stage of the process and how the different stages are connected. First, the value-adding activities are divided into two groups: primary and support activities (see below). The next step is to identify "cost drivers"—anything that affects the cost of an activity or process, such as labor hours—and determine whether costs can be reduced without adverse effects on other activities. The third step is to identify "differentiation" activities, such as improved product quality, innovation, and marketing, all of which add value to the product and give it a competitive edge. The analysis can show how each activity can be enhanced (or eliminated, if necessary) to add value.

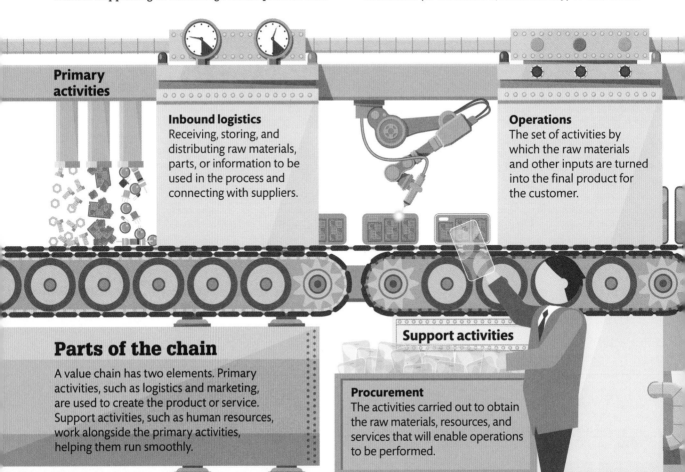

Primary activities

Inbound logistics
Receiving, storing, and distributing raw materials, parts, or information to be used in the process and connecting with suppliers.

Operations
The set of activities by which the raw materials and other inputs are turned into the final product for the customer.

Support activities

Parts of the chain

A value chain has two elements. Primary activities, such as logistics and marketing, are used to create the product or service. Support activities, such as human resources, work alongside the primary activities, helping them run smoothly.

Procurement
The activities carried out to obtain the raw materials, resources, and services that will enable operations to be performed.

✓ NEED TO KNOW

> **The sales margin** is the amount of money made after deducting direct costs from the sales price of a product or service.

> **The return on assets** is a way of calculating the profitability of a company based on its assets.

> **A cost driver** is a factor that causes the cost of an activity or process to rise or fall.

> **The differentiation advantage** is the extent to which a product or service is better than that of a competitor.

"If it doesn't add value, it's waste".

Henry Ford, Founder of
Ford Motor Company, c.1920s

Marketing and sales
Advertising, pricing, and promotion activities to sell the product or service and to attract buyers away from competitors. These may also include after-sales care.

Outbound logistics
All the activities to do with delivering the product or service to customers; these may include connecting with external transportation, storage, or fulfillment companies.

Services
The activities that are needed to keep the product working for the buyer after it is sold and delivered—such as technical support or software updates.

Human resource management
Activities to recruit, train, develop, and retain workers (or dismiss them if necessary).

Technology and infrastructure
Equipment and technological procedures used in operations, plus supportive functions such as legal, finance, and accounting.

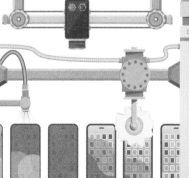

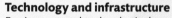

Lean Production

The goal of lean production is to identify and deliver what the customer wants from a product. This enables managers to direct their team and resources toward maximizing productivity and minimizing waste.

Establishing value

Lean production involves first identifying what the end customer values from a particular product or service, which in turn influences what the customer is prepared to pay for it. This enables managers and teams to refine the "value stream"—all the activities that go into making and delivering a product. All "non-value-adding" activities, such as warehousing unsold products, are eliminated. The results include faster and more efficient processes and higher-quality products.

Lean production was pioneered in the early 1900s by Henry Ford but was brought to its peak by Japanese car manufacturer Toyota. The system relies on a constant flow throughout a process and constant communication between those involved to refine the process.

> "People don't go to **Toyota** to **work**; they go there to **think**."
>
> Taiichi Ohno, engineer and founder of Toyota Production System, 1978

A lean machine

In the 1950s, Toyota reduced lean operations to five principles to make car manufacturing as efficient as possible. It also identified seven types of waste that should be avoided, and it has since added an eighth—namely, underused talent. Toyota's goal remains to maximize value while reducing all kinds of waste.

1. Identify value
Find out what the customer most values from a process or product.

2. Map value stream
Define the flow of activities from beginning to end of a process, to eliminate any "non-value-added" activities.

Types of waste

DEFECTS
Labor and resources wasted on a service that fails to meet customer expectations

OVERPRODUCTION
Items produced surplus to customer demand

WAITING
Unproductive time waiting for the next step in the process

UNDERUSED TALENT
Underutilization of workers' skills and knowledge

KAIZEN

KAI

改

CHANGE

ZEN

善

GOOD

Kaizen is a concept that originated in the Japanese manufacturing industry after World War II. It became popular due to its focus on producing high-quality goods at low costs. Meaning "good change," kaizen demands that managers make small but constant improvements to the working environment in order to increase productivity and effectiveness. It also encourages employees to suggest ways in which working life can be improved, both on the production line and in the company more broadly. The kaizen philosophy has had a huge impact on Japanese business, particularly in the field of "just-in-time" manufacturing. Today, for example, Toyota assembles cars in a matter of hours.

3. Create flow
Organize value-creating steps into a harmonized sequence so process flows smoothly to deliver product to customer.

4. Establish pull
Start each new activity only when there is a demand for it from the customer or from workers at the next stage of the process.

5. Seek perfection
Continue to refine process until perfect value is created with no waste.

TRANSPORTATION
Time, resources, and money wasted in moving products and materials unnecessarily

INVENTORY
Excess stock of raw materials and finished goods

OVERPROCESSING
Reworking of product, or producing goods of higher specification than required

MOTION
Time and effort wasted due to poor workflow

Meeting Objectives

Setting objectives, actioning them, then monitoring how successfully they are being achieved is a core function in any organization. There are two strategic models that managers can use.

Guided by goals

The management by objectives (MBO) model was developed in the 1950s by Peter Drucker, while Robert Kaplan and David Norton introduced the balanced scorecard (BSC) in the 1990s. The aim of MBO is to improve performance by setting clearly defined goals—agreed on by managers and their staff—that depend on the organization's vision and mission. By involving employees in planning and defining goals, managers foster empowerment and engagement, too.

How the two models work together

The MBO model can be used in conjunction with, or to inform, the BSC framework, because both models are about succeeding through defining a strategy and setting objectives. For instance, the MBO model can be used to set objectives, which are then measured using the BSC model. Alternatively, the four perspectives of the BSC model might be used to help set the objectives of the MBO model.

1. Review the organization's objectives and define goals within a specific review period.

2. Agree on employee's objectives, based on the organization's goals by using SMART objectives (see pp.148–149).

3. Monitor progress in the department.

4. Evaluate the performance of the department.

5. Reward employees for achieving their objectives.

Applying management by objectives

Managers set and review objectives for a specific period. This model works on a rewards basis, so individuals are recognized for achieving objectives.

The MBO model means business and employee performance are manageable internally, while clients or stakeholders can measure success externally.

Measuring how goals are met

The BSC model is a performance measurement tool widely used to assist in translating mission and vision statements into operational actions and to assess how MBO is working. Managers do not normally use BSC to assess individual performance but to check team performance against the business strategy. By examining four measurable areas of business—customer perception, internal business processes, financial perspective, and learning and growth—but keeping the company vision in mind at all times, BSC reveals how objectives are being met, and highlights where changes and improvements can be made. Using BSC and MBO together enables managers to both align and implement measurable objectives with their teams.

Applying the balanced scorecard

Managers use the organization's mission statement as the basis to complete a scorecard for each of the four measurable areas, specifying objectives, targets, and initiatives that can turn the company's goals into action.

Customer perception
is how a company wants to appear to its customers in order to achieve its mission.

Use the organization's mission, vision, and strategy
to assess the four measurable areas of the business.

Internal business processes
are internal practices that add value and are needed to ensure that shareholders and customers are satisfied.

Learning and growth
is a company's ability to educate itself and innovate so that it keeps changing and improving.

Financial perspective
is based on past performance and assesses the long-term viability of the chosen strategy in monetary terms.

Key Performance Indicators

Key performance indicators (KPIs) provide a framework for managers to monitor how well specific areas within their organization are functioning, and to identify potential improvements.

Understanding KPIs

In order to use KPIs, the manager must first identify the areas within the organization that contribute to its success, such as manufacturing and sales. Measurable performance targets are set for each area, then monitored at regular intervals—weekly, monthly, or quarterly. To assess how well each area is performing, the manager should compare the results that were achieved with the targets set. By doing this, the manager gains a clear understanding of which areas of the organization are performing well and where attention should be focused in order to immediately address any weaknesses. When performed over long periods, KPIs can also help the manager identify performance trends to either take advantage of or help prevent in the future.

Tracking targets

To assess the performance of his restaurant, Marco identified six aspects of the business that were essential to its success, including customer satisfaction, sales, and delivery time. After setting targets for each area, he asked his senior staff to find ways to meet the targets, and to record their progress and report the results each week. At the end of the quarter, Marco was able to identify which areas of the business had performed consistently and which ones required improvement.

"What gets measured gets managed."

VF Ridgway, US administrative scientist, 1956

8/10

7/10

CUSTOMER SATISFACTION
Marco wanted 10 positive online reviews each month.

DELIVERY TIME
Takeaway orders were to be delivered within half an hour—70 percent were.

HOW TO SET KPIS

KPIs can be used in any type of organization, although to give meaningful results, they should be applied only to the areas that contribute to its success. Managers therefore need to be specific, deciding exactly where and how to use KPIs within their organization. It is also important that the targets a manager sets are realistic and achievable. If targets are set too high, the organization is more likely to miss them, giving a false impression of its true potential performance. When setting KPIs, a manager must ensure they have:

> **A title and purpose** describing what is being measured and why.
> **Targets** that are flexible but achievable within a time frame.
> **A formula** to ensure that measurements are made in the same way each time, such as calculating a percentage.
> **A frequency** that sets how often the indicator is measured and reviewed.
> **A person or team** responsible for measuring and taking action.

✓ NEED TO KNOW

> **KPIs must align** with the organization's goals and strategy.
> **Accurate data** is essential for KPIs to be valid and effective.
> **Reliable data** must be attainable for each KPI area.
> **Communicating** KPI targets encourages the desired outcome.
> **KPIs should evolve** as the organization's performance changes over time.

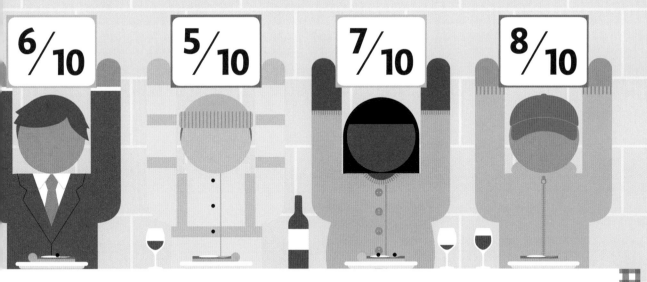

6/10

5/10

7/10

8/10

FOOD SALES
Sales were to increase 5 percent each month. Marco needs to address this area.

FOOD WASTE
Marco hoped to reduce waste by 25 percent. This remains an area of concern.

UPSELLING
Staff were asked to increase the sale of side dishes, which was successful.

STAFF SATISFACTION
Marco wants a happy team. This result pleased him.

MANAGING PEOPLE

Team Roles

Management is about building successful teams. The best teams are those in which each person's role matches their abilities and interests.

Building a team

One of a manager's responsibilities is assembling teams to carry out tasks and projects. Each team has its own function, and each team member has a particular role to play; the job of the manager is to decide which team member should do what. One method for doing this was developed by management psychologist Dr. Meredith Belbin in the 1970s and outlined in his book *Management Teams* (1981).

Nine personality types

Belbin conducted a five-year experiment to identify the types of behavior that would contribute to a high-achieving team. Although he concluded that there was no "perfect" team, he identified nine key roles, which he based on nine types of behavior.

Size matters

After five years of research, Belbin determined that the size of a team is critical to its efficiency. If a team has too many members, for example, roles can overlap, leading to confusion about who should do what. Belbin concluded that the ideal number for a team is four. This avoids any duplication of roles and promotes productive discussions and swifter decision-making. Also, while there are nine team roles in total, individuals typically have strengths in two or three areas, meaning that four people can cover all roles.

By recognizing Belbin's roles, managers can optimize their teams, recruiting members who have the personal characteristics most likely to guarantee success in a particular task. Importantly, Belbin pointed out that each of his nine roles has inherent weaknesses—for example, a creative thinker may not be a good coordinator.

PLANT

Creative and unorthodox, Plants provide the seeds for innovation, generating new ideas, and solving seemingly impenetrable problems.

MONITOR

Serious and careful in tackling problems, Monitors keep the team in check, assessing its progress and evaluating the ideas proposed by other team members.

IMPLEMENTER

Down-to-earth, practical, self-disciplined, and generally cautious, Implementers are natural administrators, able to turn a brief into a systematic plan of action.

RESOURCE INVESTIGATOR

Extroverted and curious, Resource Investigators are adept at exploring new opportunities and building relationships with external sources.

COORDINATOR

Calm, controlled, and mature, Coordinators have an overview of how a team is performing and inspire team members to stay focused on common goals.

SHAPER

Living for challenge and unafraid of confrontation, Shapers are assertive and dynamic team members, who make things happen if the group reaches an impasse.

TEAM WORKER

Readily adapting to situations and people, Team Workers are genuinely concerned with others' well-being, supporting colleagues and helping the team remain effective.

SPECIALIST

Offering extensive knowledge and expert skills in particular subject areas, Specialists act as independent advisors, lending gravitas to the team.

FINISHER

Conscientious and orderly, Finishers ensure that no detail has been overlooked, driving the team to complete the task at hand.

"Do you want a collection of brilliant minds or a brilliant collection of minds?"

Dr. Meredith Belbin

Personality Types

Assembling well-balanced teams can be a challenge for any manager. Understanding the personalities of individual staff members helps to maximize cooperation and minimize conflict.

Using personality tests
Identifying personality traits among personnel is a standard procedure at many medium and large organizations. Psychometric testing—often in the form of an detailed questionnaire that probes an individual's perception of themselves and how they might respond in particular scenarios—can also be used as a screening method to

Myers-Briggs

One of the most influential personality testing models, the Myers-Briggs Type Indicator® categorizes individuals into one of 16 different character types. To determine which type a person is most closely aligned with, they are assessed against four pairs of "opposing" qualities: extroversion–introversion; intuiting–sensing; thinking–feeling; and judging–perceiving. A questionnaire indicates whether an individual is an extrovert (E) or an introvert (I), an intuiter (N) or a senser (S), a thinker (T) or a feeler (F), and a judger (J) or a perceiver (P). On the basis of this they are accorded an overall personality type. For example, someone who has the characteristics ENFJ is designated a Teacher, whereas the characteristics ISTJ designate an Inspector.

"The best-adjusted people are the 'psychologically patriotic', who are glad to be what they are."

Isabel Briggs Myers, *Gifts Differing: Understanding Personality Type*, 1980

ENFJ

TEACHER
Organized, change-making

INFJ

COUNSELOR
Creative, nurturing, insightful

ENFP

CHAMPION
Energetic, passionate

INFP

HEALER
Idealistic, future-focused

ESFP

PERFORMER
Charming, fun-loving

ISFP

COMPOSER
Flexible, spontaneous

ESFJ

PROVIDER
Attuned to the feelings of others

ISFJ

PROTECTOR
Industrious, caring

assess attributes such as intelligence and aptitude when candidates apply for positions.

Assessing personnel

The most popular personality tests include Myers-Briggs (see below), the Big Five, DISC, HEXACO, OPQ32, and Hogan's Motive, Values, and Preferences Inventory (MVPI). These aim to provide managers with a thorough understanding of team members' personalities, enabling them to maximize individual productivity, team efficiency, and overall success. They can also be invaluable in helping managers to better understand themselves. Team members can also be tested to assess their suitability for promotions and other roles within an organization. There are various online sources for these tests, many of which produce scores that enable managers to compare the relative strengths of personnel.

INTJ

MASTERMIND
Innovative, problem-solving

ENTJ

COMMANDER
Change-embracing, sociable

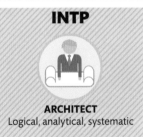

INTP

ARCHITECT
Logical, analytical, systematic

ENTP

VISIONARY
Innovative, inspirational

ISTP

CRAFTER
Observant, practical, problem-solving

ESTP

DYNAMO
Energetic, dynamic, conflict-managing

ISTJ

INSPECTOR
Neat, process-driven

ESTJ

SUPERVISOR
Hardworking, group-orientated

EXTROVERT OR INTROVERT?

Evaluating extroversion and introversion is one of the primary ways of classifying individuals. According to a 2016 analysis of BBC data by the Sutton Trust, highly extroverted workers are 25 percent more likely to be high earners. However, a 2010 study by the management school at the University of Pennsylvania found that introverted leaders were more likely to deliver better outcomes than extroverts.

Extrovert characteristics

❭ Assertive, charismatic, appear to be natural leaders
❭ Energized by interacting with people, friends, or strangers
❭ Socially active with peers and employees
❭ Excellent at bouncing ideas off others during the work day
❭ Prone to feeling threatened by others taking initiative
❭ More likely to volunteer for committees and other extra jobs

Introvert characteristics

❭ More reluctant to sell themselves
❭ Excellent listeners
❭ Good at drawing energy from ideas, images, and thoughts
❭ Able to make deep connections with people
❭ Happy to let team members take the initiative

Competencies

A competency is an ability required for a specific job. Managers need to be able to define and assess employees' competencies to ensure that they have the right people doing the right jobs.

Types of competencies

Goals or targets define *what* an employee is required to do. By contrast, competencies reveal *how* employees achieve their goals—for example, whether the person is good at problem solving, works well within a team, or perseveres in the face of challenges.

Competencies encompass many areas, from basics such as literacy to task-specific technical skills and knowledge, professional qualifications, and personal traits and behaviors such as self-motivation. Desired competencies can vary according to the employee's role and often differ by industry. For example, the competencies required of a hospital manager may differ from those required by a manager of a stockbroking firm, or from those of a more junior team member in the same organization.

Competencies can be grouped into two main types—core and functional. Core competencies are skills that are valued in most organizations as well as personal traits that align with the workplace culture. Functional competencies are job-related skills, which are often measurable and defined by specific qualifications.

By defining core and functional competencies, managers can clarify what is expected in specific roles and align individual or team activities with the organization's overall purpose and values. These definitions can be used to recruit job applicants and guide the development of employees.

Regulatory compliance

Certification to sho[w] compliance with he[alth &] safety, environment[al and] other regulation[s]

Relevant qualifications

Evidence of experience and/or training, such as academic or industry qualifications

FROM INTELLIGENCE TO COMPETENCY

In 1973, David McClelland published an influential paper in the journal *American Psychologist* arguing that testing for intelligence, or IQ, was less effective than testing a person's competence in managing real life—including practical, interpersonal, and leadership skills. McClelland drew on research showing that academic achievement at school was not a reliable predictor of job performance. He focused on finding out how a successful worker thinks and acts and how to develop their competencies. His ideas formed the basis of the contemporary business focus on identifying competencies and testing for them during the recruitment process.

Defining competencies

When creating a job description for a certain role, it is useful to outline a list of desired competencies for prospective job applicants. Managers need to define a few core competencies (see examples, right) indicating that an employee is appropriate for the role and will help fulfill the organization's goals. The description should also specify the applicant's required competencies (see above) and define their expected performance level.

Technical skills

Evidence of technical knowledge, such as a certificate from a training course

Up-to-date knowledge

Evidence of keeping abreast of developments in the relevant industry or work environment

Track record

Evidence of previous success in the field of work, such as a portfolio of completed projects

✓ NEED TO KNOW

> **Hard skills** are formally acquired, quantifiable indicators of ability, such as a certificate or degree. These skills come under functional competencies.

> **Soft skills** are personal, cognitive, and behavioral abilities, such as communication skills, critical thinking, and problem-solving. These fall in the group of core competencies.

> **Transversal skills**, also known as transferable skills, can be applied to a wide variety of jobs. These include basics such as literacy and numeracy and fundamental personal skills such as the ability to work well with others.

CORE COMPETENCIES

- **Teamwork:** the ability to collaborate and communicate effectively with coworkers
- **Decision-making:** effective responses to challenges
- **Good work ethic:** resilience, self-motivation, tenacity
- **Thinking skills:** analytical thinking, innovative ideas

93%

of all employers say that critical thinking, clear thinking, and problem-solving abilities are more important than a job applicant's degree major

Association of American Colleges and Universities, 2013

Finding and Selecting Talent

Hiring the right people is central for building a successful team. Managers need to plan the process to ensure that they choose those with the appropriate personal and professional skills.

Initial planning

An effective recruitment and selection process has several steps, from identifying a role to be filled to employing the new candidate and integrating them into the team.

The first stage is to carry out a job analysis of the role. To define the core functions and necessary skills, current employees in similar roles are asked about their main tasks and the intended outcome of their work. This information is used to outline the qualities and skills that candidates should possess.

Next, managers and coworkers of the new person need to plan the recruitment process. Tasks involve drafting a job description; deciding where and how to advertise the post; deciding on the elements of the interview process, including whether to carry out preinterview screening by phone and who will sit on the interview panel; and compiling questions for use in prescreening and the interview itself.

THE RECRUITMENT PROCESS

Finding and retaining the right employees requires careful recruitment planning.

> **Advertise** positions both internally and externally.

> **Promote** the organization's values so that applicants are aware of the organization's philosophy.

> **Schedule** interviews close together for ease of comparing candidates.

> **Check** the candidates' backgrounds and consult their references.

> **Ensure** that candidates know whether an offer is conditional (i.e., subject to further testing) or unconditional.

> **Set up** induction processes to help new employees settle into the workplace.

Fishing for talent

Just because an organization advertises a job vacancy, it does not mean that the best candidates will apply, or then take the role if it is offered. People have a choice over where they work, so in order to appeal to the best talent, the organization and role must seem attractive. Managers must promote the wider benefits of the organization to candidates, such as rewarding work, and structured career progression.

INSPIRING MISSION

CAREER DEVELOPMENT

EXCITING PROJECTS

Interviewing

Once all the applications are in, the résumés are reviewed. It may be helpful to use prescreening to select a "long list" of applicants who will be invited to interview.

The interviewer or panel needs to decide in advance who will ask questions on which topics. To assess applicants equally, a checklist should be drafted, including questions on personal as well as technical capabilities. A skills test or a personality test may also be helpful. After the interviews, those involved should meet to discuss the applicants.

BEHAVIORAL INTERVIEWING

This technique is based on the idea that how someone has behaved in the past is the best predictor of how they will behave in the future. Some sample questions illustrating the technique are given below.

✓ **Do ask:** How did you go about training a supervisor?	✗ **Do not ask:** Have you ever trained a supervisor?
✓ **Do ask:** Have you ever faced a dissatisfied client?	✗ **Do not ask:** What would you do if a client threatened to leave?
✓ **Do ask:** How did you implement change management in your previous job?	✗ **Do not ask:** How would you implement change management in our department?

CONGENIAL CULTURE · CLEAR EXPECTATIONS · SHARING OF IDEAS · EQUAL OPPORTUNITIES · CREATIVE OUTLETS · SOCIAL ACTIVITIES

Benefits of Diversity

Everyone within an organization has different ideas and experience to offer. When managed well, this creates a valuable synergy that enables diverse organizations to outperform their non-diverse counterparts.

Managing a diverse team

In today's workplace, most companies have diversity policies and programs. They do so not only to meet equal-opportunity standards but also to enhance productivity, since a diverse environment encourages creativity. However, there are challenges in harmonizing the different personalities, values, and cultural attitudes of a diverse team, and facing

Being inclusive

Just as a garden is more bountiful and vibrant when it has a mixture of different plants, a diverse workplace is often a more productive one. For a manager, the key to achieving a diverse workplace is the use of a bias-free recruitment and selection process and company policies that encourage inclusivity.

Recruitment
Inclusive recruitment starts with informed advertising, which should be targeted to encourage the widest range of applicants.

Selection process
Mechanisms to ensure bias-free recruitment include removing all personal information from candidates' applications.

these challenges is a key task for a manager. The goal is to respect individuals' differences while at the same time encouraging what they have in common.

Leading an effective team, therefore, involves balancing the needs of both the group and the individuals within it—and this requires managers to ensure that their personal values do not interfere with team dynamics. Studies have also shown that diversity among managers leads to greater innovation and higher revenues for their companies. This has led to companies seeking diversity throughout their staff as well as providing on-the-job diversity training.

Diverse companies outperform industry norms by
35%

McKinsey & Company, management consultants, 2015

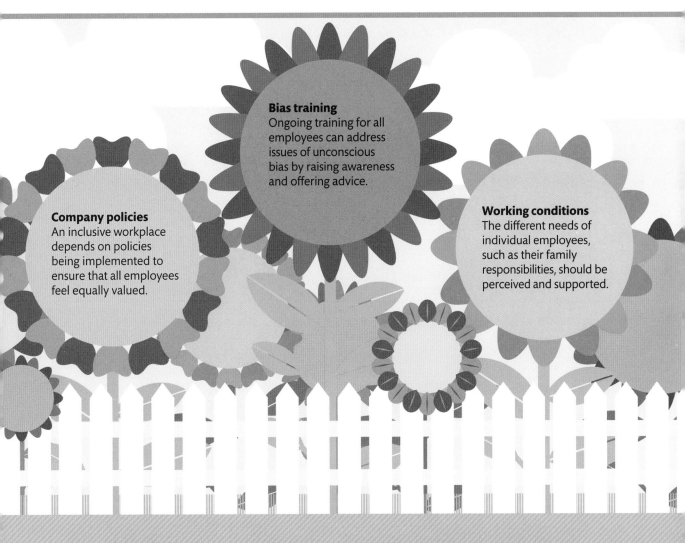

Bias training
Ongoing training for all employees can address issues of unconscious bias by raising awareness and offering advice.

Company policies
An inclusive workplace depends on policies being implemented to ensure that all employees feel equally valued.

Working conditions
The different needs of individual employees, such as their family responsibilities, should be perceived and supported.

Workplace Well-being

From upgrading furniture and equipment to monitoring workloads, there are many ways in which a manager can boost employee well-being and foster a happier, healthier, and more committed workforce.

Well-being initiatives

Ensuring that a workplace is both appealing and functions optimally is increasingly a priority for managers who want to keep staff positive and engaged. A well-designed workplace reduces the risk of accidents, illness, and stress-related health problems. Ergonomics—the science of tailoring products and systems to the end user—can help managers achieve this. Ergonomics covers three areas: physical ergonomics—designing furniture and devices to suit a user's anatomy without imposing strain on any part of the body; cognitive ergonomics—ensuring that devices and systems are user-friendly; and organizational ergonomics—setting up structures, policies, and work practices that foster manageable workloads.

Well-being initiatives, often led by HR managers, vary according to the company but they can include health insurance, user-friendly working areas, risk assessments, fair and open remuneration, and a management style that involves staff in decision-making and ensures that their voice is heard.

Designing the work environment

A workplace that is bright, safe, comfortabl and fully functional safeguards employee health and promotes well-being. In a thoughtfully planned work environment, every aspect, from machines to air quality, is tailored to the tasks required and the benefit of the staff who carry them out. Companies that have addressed these issues report higher productivity, less absenteeism, and increased staff retention.

 NEED TO KNOW

> **Anthropometry is** the science of measuring the body and its proportions, used in the design of work stations, for example.

> **Participatory ergonomics means** actively involving employees in developing and implementing workplace changes.

> **Human-factors engineering is** a discipline that takes into account human strengths and limitations when interactive devices, systems, and structures are designed.

> **Psychosocial risk management** is concerned with examining workloads, work conditions, and working methods to reduce the likelihood of mental health issues.

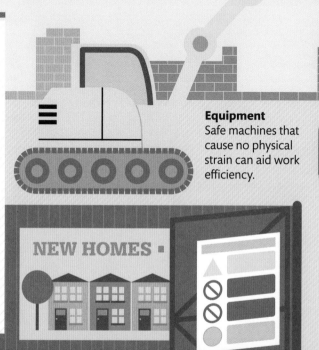

Equipment
Safe machines that cause no physical strain can aid work efficiency.

Workload
Monitoring and adjusting workloads can ensure that employees are able to manage their tasks without stress.

Doubling ventilation rates can increase cognitive performance by more than

100%

Associations of Cognitive Function Scores with Carbon Dioxide, Ventilation, and Volatile Organic Compound Exposures in Office Workers, Harvard University, 2016

HOW EMPLOYEES CAN HELP

Collaborating with staff can help managers to:

> **Identify** workplace risks.
> **Ensure** that health and safety controls are practical.
> **Gain** employee commitment to working in a safe, healthy way.

Vision
Free eye tests and ensuring screen displays are optimized protects sight.

Lighting
Well-designed lighting will reduce eye strain and ensure that staff can perform their work efficiently.

Air
Filtered air, good ventilation, and adjustable temperature settings support employee well-being.

Software
Using intuitive programs that are easy to operate helps avoid employee stress.

Workspace
To enable staff to work comfortably, workstations and work spaces must be designed to suit their needs.

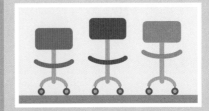

Furniture
Office furniture should support good posture and be adjustable to meet different users' needs.

Noise
Sound-masking technology can protect hearing and reduce the impact of noisy environments on productivity.

Signs
Safety signs and important notices should be in prominent positions and easy to read.

NEW HOMES ▪ N

Retaining Talent

Engaged and hardworking personnel are a huge asset to any organization. Nurturing and channeling their talents and encouraging them to stay is therefore a key part of management.

Keeping the best

Managing talented employees effectively and persuading them to give their all for as long as possible is important for any organization. Gifted and productive staff contribute to the success and future of a company and are also expensive to replace.

Good managers therefore try to keep all employees satisfied by providing encouragement and dealing swiftly with issues. However, high-achieving staff may be easily bored and require challenging tasks to keep them engaged. They may also need constructive feedback to ensure that they remain motivated. If possible, they should be given more autonomy and projects of their own—as well as financial incentives, such as a promotion or a bonus (see pp.138–139).

People stay with an organization when they feel valued. This means that managers must trust them, respect their opinions, and listen to any grievances that they may have. When valued employees do decide to leave, however, it is good practice to hold an exit interview to establish why they are going and whether anything can be done to change their minds.

Staff turnover

In today's flexible market, employees change jobs much more frequently than in the past. To avoid the high cost of replacing staff, managers should make employees feel welcome from the start. They should also set clear guidelines for the work and offer incentives to ensure that employees stay focused and motivated.

1 **Give new employees an easy first day** with a prepared workspace and a welcome lunch or drinks so that they can get to know their colleagues.

2 **Instigate a trial period** to enable new employee to settle in and for managers to assess them.

MEASURING TURNOVER

By measuring their employee turnover rate, companies can monitor the costs of losing or hiring staff. The percentage of staff leaving over a set period, such as a year, is calculated with a formula: the number of employees who left is divided by the average number of employees, and the total is multiplied by 100.

$$\frac{\text{Staff who left}}{(\text{Staff at beginning of set period} + \text{staff at end of set period}) \div 2} \times 100$$

Average worldwide staff turnover rate is

10.9%

Linkedin, 2017

4 **Motivate employees** by providing regular praise and feedback, new work challenges, and opportunities to progress within the organization.

3 **Discuss roles and responsibilities**, ensuring that employees understand their particular objectives.

6 **Invite employees who decide to leave** to complete a questionnaire or attend an exit interview to discuss their reasons, and how they might be retained.

5 **Offer financial incentives** to productive staff, such as bonuses, pay raises, promotion, or company benefits such as private health insurance.

 CASE STUDY

Zappos

At online fashion brand Zappos, retaining staff begins by recruiting the right people. Even the drivers who pick up the candidates from the airport can decide whether they are appropriate. After four weeks of paid training, new staff are offered $2,000 to leave if the company is not right for them, ensuring that all who choose to stay on are fully committed.

THE COST OF STAFF TURNOVER

Replacing an employee can cost a firm 50–60 percent of that employee's annual salary, according to the Society for Human Resource Management. When turnover is high, managers must ensure that productivity is not reduced by low morale among staff.

RECRUITING COSTS · HR COSTS · TRAINING TIME · LOW PRODUCTIVITY · LOSS OF REVENUE · LOW MORALE

Meeting Employees' Needs

Job satisfaction relies on more than a good wage. People perform better at work if their emotional and psychological needs are met too.

Understanding individuals

Successful managers understand what motivates each of their team members. This is the key to ensuring that they stay focused, maintain company loyalty, and achieve business targets. One of the best-known explanations of what motivates behavior is American psychologist Abraham Maslow's "hierarchy of needs," which helps managers identify what each of their team members needs in order to perform well.

The hierarchy of needs

In 1943, Maslow published his paper "A Theory of Human Motivation", which he described as a hierarchy of needs: the things that drive humans to act in order to satisfy those needs. His idea can be visualized as a pyramid, starting at the bottom with a person's basic needs, and working up to emotional and spiritual needs, as each level is satisfied.

✓ NEED TO KNOW

❯ **Not everyone prioritizes** their needs in the same order, and self-actualization is not everyone's goal, so the hierarchy may need to be adapted for different people.

❯ **Maslow's hierarchy** was based on behavioral studies in the US, but as behaviors vary between countries, managers should be sensitive to cultural differences.

❯ **It is difficult to measure** satisfaction at each level since many of the needs are emotional, and so subjective.

5 Life goals
Provide guidance, foster career paths, and take real interest in each employee as a person.

Self-actualization
Having grown and developed on a spiritual level, a person can achieve a sense of personal fulfillment.

4 Well done!
Encourage employees and reward good work with praise and recognition.

X AND Y FACTORS

Two alternative views of what motivates people to work were developed by US management professor Douglas McGregor. Theory X assumes employees do not really want to work and have to be enticed to do so with rewards or punished for not working. This requires a hands-on management style. Theory Y assumes employees are self-motivated and work to better themselves, so they are best managed by encouraging creativity.

Esteem
When a person is recognized by others for their achievements, they begin to feel good about themselves, helping build self-esteem.

3 Build morale
Cultivate a positive attitude within the team; encourage diversity and personal friendships.

Love and belonging
People like to feel as though they are part of a group—they need to build close relationships and have a sense of being accepted and cared for.

2 Secure future
Pay employees adequately and provide a safe, stable, and clean working environment.

Safety
Having a secure home to shelter in and a stable work environment help make a person feel safe in the company of strangers or acquaintances.

1 Comfort
Offer employees breaks, reasonable working hours, and comfortable conditions.

Physiological
A person's most basic needs relate to survival: having air to breathe; having food, water, warmth, sleep, and somewhere to shelter; and being able to reproduce.

Motivation and Reward

Skilled managers cultivate dynamic and loyal teams by listening to their views, recognizing their value, rewarding success, and removing factors that decrease motivation.

Keeping staff motivated

Employees with motivation show it through their commitment and effort in the workplace. Most companies aim to encourage these people, and less engaged staff, with a program that rewards hard work, progress, and success.

There are two types of rewards: tangible rewards, such as salary increases, promotions, and bonuses; and intangible rewards, such as praise, interesting and challenging work, and the hope of career development. The department manager will decide how to apply the program to each team member, directly influencing whether that member is motivated or not. A good manager always uses intangible rewards and applies tangible ones where possible. Failure to motivate team members will result in high staff turnover and reduced productivity.

Different employees value different rewards. Some may want to reach management level; others might value positive feedback or more responsibility within their role. An effective manager chooses the most suitable reward for each person, making clear the link between reward and performance.

Herzberg's two-factor motivation theory

Published in 1958, US psychologist Frederick Herzberg's two-factor motivation theory divided factors that influence employee engagement into "motivators" and "hygiene factors". He argued that motivators, such as achievement, recognition, and responsibility, have great potential to increase engagement. However, unless hygiene factors, such as poor pay, low status, and job insecurity, are eliminated, staff will be disengaged no matter how good the motivators are.

ENGAGEMENT AND MORALE

Managers should recognize whether staff are engaged or not. Disengaged staff tend to be less productive and spread poor morale. They are also more likely to resign.

> **Engaged employees** work with pride, project positivity toward colleagues, and feel connected to the company. They help drive innovation and profitability.

> **Employees who are not engaged** fulfill their core responsibilities but do not seem to have passion and energy.

> **Actively disengaged employees** express their unhappiness and dissatisfaction to coworkers on a daily basis, bringing down team morale.

Motivated employees are

21%
more productive and

22%
more profitable than unmotivated staff

Gallup Q12 survey, 2016

MOTIVATORS

Rewarding work

Employees feel motivated if work is interesting, challenging, rewarding, and worthwhile.

Achievement

Managers can create a sense of achievement by setting clear goals and encouraging the staff to take pride in their work.

Praise and recognition

Praise, positive feedback, and recognition of success can increase job satisfaction and motivate employees.

Responsibility and autonomy

A good manager should not "micromanage" but allow employees responsibility for their work.

Growth and experience

Opportunities for growth and personal development are important motivating factors.

Career development

Many workers, particularly junior staff or those aspiring to management roles, will feel motivated if promoted.

HYGIENE FACTORS

Low status

Unmotivated employees may not feel valued or that their work is meaningful.

Poor conditions

Long working hours and poor facilities or equipment can reduce motivation.

Job insecurity

Staff are less likely to engage with their work if they feel they are at risk of losing their job.

Unfair pay

Staff will feel disengaged if their pay does not reflect their performance.

Bad working relationships

Poor relations among staff or between staff and managers are demotivating.

Team Development

Nurturing the skills of a team and helping it grow, meet challenges, and deliver results is a crucial managerial process. Done well, it boosts morale, binds the team, and encourages good performance.

Making the most of teams

Whenever a manager takes over an existing team or forms a new one to complete a task or project, the process of team development should begin. It means assembling the team and helping members integrate, work together, face challenges, solve problems, and deliver results. It also involves nurturing talent and recognizing and addressing individual needs.

Behavioral psychologists have identified the key stages of putting a team together, from the initial team meeting to the delivery of a project. One of the best-known illustrations of this process is the forming, storming, norming, and performing (FSNP) model, first proposed by American psychological researcher Bruce Tuckman in 1965 (see below). When team members are also made aware of the process,

managers can encourage them to observe their own behavior and understand their experiences.

Developing the talents of individual team members is equally important. Proven strategies (see box, right), such as providing regular feedback, delegating new duties, or providing team members with support materials or a mentor, encourage employees to perform at their best.

The FSNP model

The FSNP model illustrates the key stages of the team development process. At each stage, a manager can use various techniques to steer the process along the right path. This model still forms the basis of contemporary practice in many organizations.

FORMING

Individuals come together and get to know one another. They build trust and learn about the task ahead, including challenges and opportunities. Managers should:

❯ **Break the ice** with a social gathering.
❯ **Consider trust-building** exercises.
❯ **Provide a clear brief** with defined roles.

STORMING

Relationships develop, members begin to voice ideas, and some may jostle for power. In this phase, the team needs strong leadership from managers, who should:

❯ **Identify potential conflict** and intervene sensitively.
❯ **Provide clear leadership** to stay fixed on goals.
❯ **Be prepared to support** individual members.

✓ NEED TO KNOW

> **Adjourning** is the final stage in the FSNP model, which Tuckman added later. It refers to the team disbanding, perhaps at the end of a project. Some members may feel unsettled by this stage approaching.

> **Swift trust** refers to the rapid formation of working relationships in teams, most commonly virtual, where there is no time to develop a sense of mutual trust before starting work on the task.

NURTURING THE TEAM

Managers can help staff progress by conducting regular reviews and offering them chances to develop by:

> **Providing a buddy** for new starters
> **Scheduling coaching** sessions
> **Giving opportunities** to work alongside more experienced colleagues
> **Delegating tasks** that are more challenging
> **Facilitating moves** to other parts of the organization to learn new skills
> **Providing a mentor** for career development
> **Organizing training** courses for professional development
> **Encouraging membership** of relevant professional bodies

"Coming together is a beginning, staying together is progress, and working together is success."

Henry Ford, founder of Ford Motor Company

NORMING

The team finds equilibrium as members work together smoothly, each taking responsibility for their role and staying focused on success. Managers should:

> **Hold regular feedback** sessions to check progress.
> **Be alert to complacency** by noticing its early signs.
> **Encourage** and reward small successes.

PERFORMING

Team members are now seizing the initiative and taking greater responsibility. As the team now requires less direction, managers may:

> **Refrain from interfering** unnecessarily and let the team get on with their work.
> **Permit a degree of challenge**; this is not a problem if members respect one another's opinions, and it can lead to innovation.
> **Identify talents in individuals** who could be assisted in their career-path progression.

SMART Management

Before assigning a task to a team member, it is vital to define the key aims. Setting SMART objectives ensures that the task stays on track.

Setting objectives

Initiatives like Peter Drucker's management by objectives (see pp.122–123) are effective ways of helping a company achieve its business goals. They involve setting objectives and creating processes to meet them. But for day-to-day tasks, SMART planning is more useful. Standing for specific, measurable, achievable, realistic, and time-based, it was developed by US consultant George T. Doran in 1981. Its simple approach was intended to aid managers confused by the plethora of advice available.

Doran stated that to be effective, an objective does not have to meet all five criteria; however, the closer it comes to meeting them all, the "smarter" it is.

After setting SMART objectives, it is vital to develop a specific plan of action to achieve them.

SMART planning

The simplicity of the SMART approach has made it one of the most popular tools for setting and achieving objectives. By requiring that each of an organization's objectives is measured against the five criteria, SMART enables managers and team members to approach tasks in a consistent way. It also reduces the risk of setting goals that are vague, hard to measure, or may ultimately never be met.

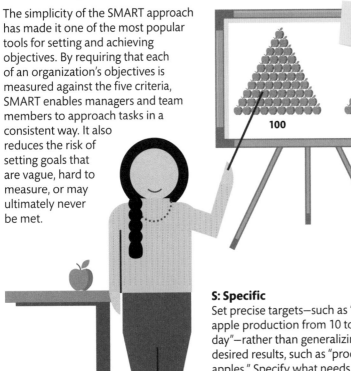

S: Specific
Set precise targets—such as "increase apple production from 10 to 100 per day"—rather than generalizing about desired results, such as "produce more apples." Specify what needs to be accomplished, why it is important, who is involved, where it will occur, and what resources are available.

M: Measurable
Ensure that objectives are quantifiable so that the success of the task can be assessed once it is completed. In other words, ensure that a measurement system is in place—for example, recording the numbers of apples picked per day—and measure at the start of the task and again at the end.

> ## "Objectives and... action plans are the most critical steps in a company's management process."
> George T. Doran

GOALS AND OBJECTIVES

Business management experts have often discussed the differences between goals and objectives.

Goals	*Objectives*
❯ Conceptual statements	❯ Specific steps for reaching goals
❯ Relate to the big picture for the organization	❯ Usually quantifiable and measurable
❯ Employ emotive language	❯ Employ factual language
❯ Define the direction that managers intend a business to take	❯ Motivational, as achieving goals boosts morale of team members
❯ Express aspirations	❯ Support long-term goals
❯ Often continuous and long term	❯ Often short term, especially on a departmental level

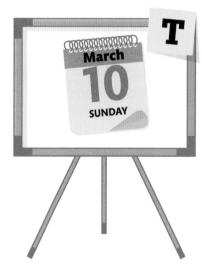

A: Achievable
Question whether the group has the necessary skills to achieve an objective. For example, the apple business might require expert horticulturists who are able to increase production because they have the skills and expertise to cultivate the fruit trees.

R: Realistic
Ensure that the entire task is possible. Question whether results can be achieved given the current constraints and conditions. For example, if the lease on the orchard land is about to expire, it is unrealistic to pursue expansion without first renegotiating the lease.

T: Time-based
Set a time frame for the objective to be achieved. The existing apple trees need to be pruned in winter to generate an increased crop the following summer. It may take two years to achieve a large increase in yield and hence production, so ensure this is taken into consideration.

Developing Trust

Hard to earn but easy to lose, trust is a fundamental part of building and maintaining a professional reputation. Understanding how it works underpins every aspect of management.

Actions, not words

As in all areas of life, managers do not win trust by what they say but earn it through what they do and how they act. According to workplace surveys, employees expect their bosses to behave with honesty and transparency and act responsibly.

First, managers must be seen to trust their employees and show that they are willing to stand by their word. It is important to foster trust between the members of a team and between employees and the company. A manager should also consider how ethical their own behavior is and how consistently it is observed and experienced by others within the workplace.

Establishing trust between the manager and their team, and within the team, will also have a positive effect on the success of an organization. The employees are not only more likely to be engaged and productive at work but also to trust, and be advocates for, their organization. Trust can be achieved by encouraging employees to talk, using trust-building exercises, and setting an example by always being honest and talking openly about difficult situations.

A delicate balance

The more trust employees have in one another and in their managers, the stronger and more productive a team will be. A manager who conducts business and personal affairs ethically, communicates openly with their employees about what is happening within the organization and how well team members are performing, and admits to making mistakes is more likely to be deemed trustworthy. Here are some ways in which managers can build mutual trust in the workplace.

CASE STUDY

Hewlett-Packard

In 1998, Hewlett-Packard made *Fortune* magazine's list of 100 best companies to work for. But in 1999, a new management team called for a drastic change in strategy, despite good performance to date, which left employees feeling unappreciated. When business declined, employees were asked to take pay cuts with a promise of no redundancies—but 6,000 jobs were lost. A merger with computer giant Compaq in 2001 cost yet more jobs and was deemed to put an end to HP's tradition of putting people and principles first.

30%
of employees do not trust the company they work for

Edelman Trust Barometer, 2016

Deal with issues responsibly—a manager's reputation is made or broken during a crisis.

Demonstrate social awareness by encouraging measures that will benefit those in need.

Talk about personal values and past mistakes, but beware of sharing too much information.

Be transparent—admit to making mistakes rather than covering them up.

Demonstrate trust in your employees—they will feel you do not trust them if you watch their every move.

Avoid office gossip by taking a neutral stance—do not engage with rumors or acrimonious comments.

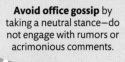

Empower team members by communicating honestly on the state of the organization.

Give and accept feedback, be honest and constructive and allow team members to have their say, too.

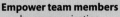

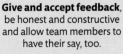

Dealing with Staff Conflict

Even in well-run teams, moments of conflict can arise. The key to managing them is to recognize the early signs and put strategies in place before minor disagreements turn into something more serious.

Monitoring and understanding conflict

Although a manager should seek to maintain good working relations within their organization, there are still likely to be instances in which individuals, teams, or departments come head-to-head in moments of tension. If not managed, these situations can lead to full-blown battles that are potentially destructive, not only to employee morale but also to company culture and business performance. In any conflict situation, the aim is to identify the underlying causes and reach an amicable resolution. Conflicts may have sometimes been brewing for a while before a manager hears about them. Getting to know individual team members and how each person reacts to adversity helps managers recognize the early signs of conflict (see box, below). Timing is also critical—a manager who deals decisively with conflict before the situation intensifies will earn the respect of their employees. If a dispute cannot be resolved in the early stages, or the conflict involves a complaint about treatment in the workplace or company procedures, most organizations have a formal process in place for managers to follow.

TOP FIVE SIGNS OF CONFLICT

The negative effects of conflict in an organization can manifest themselves in many ways. Managers need to be able to recognize the following signs in order to prevent a situation from escalating.

> **Loss of motivation**: team members become reluctant to participate in meetings or volunteer for new tasks.

> **Withdrawal and antagonism**: staff can be heard making incendiary remarks and may take part in fewer social activities than before.

> **Drop in productivity**: reduced cooperation between employees often leads to less efficient processes and more avoidable errors.

> **Increased absence**: depression or stress at work can lead to long-term illness or apathy about going to work.

> **Negative feedback**: staff questionnaires or surveys are useful in revealing underlying discontent within an organization.

Resolving conflict

The process outlined by an organization for managing conflict usually includes both formal and informal guidelines that managers can follow. Low-level conflicts may be dealt with on a more personal basis, between a manager and team members, but escalating grievances require more official responses.

PREVENTING CONFLICT

Act quickly when a conflict is suspected to make it easier to gain evidence of wrongdoing before confronting anyone. A delay in dealing with the issue can lead to team members losing respect for their manager.

Be aware of varying boundaries between individual personalities who may each deal with conflict differently.

Offer consistent coaching to give employees the emotional skills to deal more objectively with issues, helping them steer clear of conflict.

Respect differences and avoid conflict by giving equal treatment to staff who seem different or have different values.

Prevent tension by managing workloads so that staff do not feel under stress for prolonged periods, which can lead them to become tense and ill-tempered. Talk to staff about their work.

MAJOR CONFLICT
An employment tribunal claim

FORMAL ACTION
Seek arbitration (settlement) by an independent body

MAJOR CONFLICT
A formal grievance against another employee

FORMAL ACTION
Follow company procedures for tackling grievances

MINOR CONFLICT
An ongoing problem, with signs of rivalry, stress, or resentment

INFORMAL ACTION
Discuss the situation informally with the individuals and address the underlying issues

MINOR CONFLICT
A one-off disagreement

INFORMAL ACTION
Talk to the employee, listening but not judging; keep a diary on the issue if it threatens to be ongoing

Delegation

Delegating—giving authority to a team member to carry out a specific task or role—is a core developmental tool for managers. It empowers staff with new capabilities and makes an organization more effective.

Entrusting authority

Distributing tasks among a team is a basic management principle, but to work effectively, the manager needs to delegate—handing over some of their own responsibilities and authority to a chosen other. This has a dual effect: the manager is freed up to concentrate on other tasks required by their senior role, while the chosen team member feels empowered, not only due to the trust placed in their abilities but also by the chance to reinforce and develop their skill set. In addition, the new experience and responsibility can increase their importance to their team.

Delegating responsibility to team members can be energizing as they rise to meet new challenges, and it also encourages them to take ownership of projects. By delegating a particular task to different staff members in turn, managers can enhance the overall skills and flexibility of their team.

Delegating effectively

Since the employee will be accountable for the outcome of the task or role, how the manager hands over the task is critical, as is their initial guidance. Managers must prepare the team member by encouraging them to consider relevant factors, including how to integrate the new task with existing duties.

1

Consider which team member is most suitable

❯ Who can do the task?

❯ Who is performing work they no longer find challenging and will benefit from doing this?

❯ Are they already overstretched?

❯ Will they be interested?

2

Give the employee enough authority to do the project

❯ Verify that they agree to and understand the expectations.

❯ Avoid stepping in to micromanage the employee.

❯ Stress to colleagues that the employee has a degree of autonomy.

3

Set clear objectives and guidelines

❯ Spell out any aspects of the task that are nonnegotiable.

❯ Define what they can and cannot do without permission.

❯ Give a clear schedule and set check-in times and deadlines.

❯ Allow the employee to make the task more efficient.

WHEN TO DELEGATE

Some tasks should always be dealt with by the manager, but many others can be delegated. If a manager is reluctant to hand over responsibilities, this may simply be an attitude that can be changed, rather than a genuine obstacle.

❯ **"There is no time to delegate; it is quicker to do it myself."** Although it will take time to brief a staff member, it will pay dividends later when they can more quickly understand what is needed in the future.

❯ **"No one will be able to do this task as well as I can."** While it is hard to impart experience and expertise, with the right information and training, staff can deliver. However, some tasks, such as appraisals, disciplinary action, and confidential matters, should not be delegated.

❯ **"The team member already has a lot of work; I do not want to overload them."** Although staff may be busy, this could be a chance to increase their skill set and experience.

46%
of companies are concerned about the delegation skills of staff

Institute for Corporate Productivity (i4cp), 2007

4

Be fair and reasonable

❯ Provide the employee with adequate resources to complete the task, such as a budget.

❯ Allow sufficient time for the completion of each stage.

❯ Be available to provide support or advice if the employee requires it.

5

Assess the delegate's performance

❯ Provide mentoring, especially if they are doing the task for the first time.

❯ Check in and provide constructive feedback.

❯ Recognize success at each stage and provide encouragement.

6

Stay accountable

❯ Maintain responsibility for the outcome of the project.

❯ If the employee is not delivering, retrace steps 1 to 5 and modify where needed.

❯ Avoid taking back the project if possible.

❯ Assess the outcome and provide feedback to the employee.

Big Ideas

Brainstorming sessions—in which people are encouraged to generate new ideas—can make a valuable contribution to problem-solving and innovation. When managed correctly, brainstorming can facilitate breakthrough thinking.

Successful brainstorming

Business relies on innovation, but in the normal course of work, there are limited opportunities for generating new ideas. Advertising executive Alex Osborn created the technique called "brainstorming" in 1948 after identifying that a lack of original ideas was stifling growth in some organizations. Brainstorming is a dedicated forum in which individuals can freely propose ideas, no matter how quirky. These can then be assessed, built on, or adapted.

Including diverse individuals in the group is the key to successful group brainstorming—a cross section of people from different disciplines, with varied experiences, generally results in greater creativity. Posing the right kinds of questions is also important. People will find it easier to contribute constructively if the scope of the session is focused on a problem that needs solving. During the session, the proposed ideas should all be recorded, and the most promising ones should be short-listed for follow-up.

Together or alone?

Management experts are divided over whether brainstorming solo or in a group is more effective. People sometimes generate more ideas on their own, since they are less likely to be influenced by others, while group brainstorming sessions can be beneficial for increasing engagement among team members buying in to solutions, and generating diverse ideas. However, research shows that, since the number of ideas generated per person declines as group size increases, a group limited to between five and seven is ideal. Bearing in mind these varying benefits, a combination of both approaches may deliver the best results.

> "Brainstorm means using the brain to storm a creative problem."
>
> Alex Osborn, *Your Creative Power*, 1948

INDIVIDUAL BRAINSTORMING

Techniques to free up ideas when brainstorming alone include:

> ❯ **"Free writing,"** which involves writing anything that comes to mind, for a set period of time.
> ❯ Make a **"spider diagram"** to link ideas together.

IDEAS

MOST EFFECTIVE FOR GENERATING A LARGE NUMBER OF IDEAS

CASE STUDY

3M and the 30 per cent rule

Executives at US multinational company 3M are committed to supporting ideas that emerge from brainstorming sessions. They introduced a rule that 30 percent of the revenue generated by each division must come from products created over the previous four years. This motivates employees to innovate and to come up with new products.

TOP TIPS FOR BRAINSTORMING

Creativity in brainstorming flourishes when certain limits are set at the start of the session:

❯ **Provide a clear brief** with one objective to enable a more focused approach in the session.
❯ **Maintain order** by managing the people involved and preventing any participants from dismissing the ideas of others and stifling creativity as well as ensuring that everyone participates.
❯ **Ask thought-provoking questions**, such as: "What is the biggest drawback of the company's product?", "How can we identify new markets?", or "In what ways can the company reduce costs without significantly impacting on our customers and clients?"

GROUP BRAINSTORMING

Tips for successful group sessions include:

❯ **Use an outside facilitator** so that the manager and team can focus on ideas.
❯ **Set a time limit** for the session.
❯ **Remove all possible distractions**, such as electronic devices.
❯ **Encourage participants** to generate as many ideas as possible.

❯ **Hold back from criticism**—treat all ideas as equally valid.
❯ **Prioritize unusual** or promising ideas.
❯ **Build on** and refine proposals.
❯ **Give participants a set period** after the meeting during which they can submit any further ideas.

MOST EFFECTIVE FOR GENERATING TEAM SYNERGY AND BUY-IN TO SOLUTIONS

Coaching and Mentoring

Developing employees through coaching and mentoring has become part of the fabric of modern management. It ensures that staff get the relevant training and keeps them more engaged and productive.

The manager as guide

A key aspect of good management involves guiding and training staff to ensure that they perform at their best. Coaching and mentoring, which have long existed, have become more popular in recent years and are now often part of training and development programs. Managers who have hands-on experience and on-the-job knowledge are in an excellent position to direct these types of trainings.

Coaching is generally short term and may involve the manager, another staff member, or an outside trainer teaching employees skills relevant to their work. Mentoring, often directed by the manager, is focused on building long-term knowledge and professional judgment. For management, the benefits of both types of training are that staff quickly learn the right skills for their work and develop to their full potential. A further bonus is that staff may stay longer in their posts because they feel valued.

COACHING

> **Short-term training** designed to teach new skills relevant to the employee's work.

> **Specific to a particular task** or area of work and can help staff solve immediate problems.

> **Clearly outlines what steps to take** in a real work situation the employee will encounter.

> **Produces immediate feedback** for a manager on employee performance.

Tailored training

Coaching and mentoring are different techniques with different objectives. Managers play a role in both. They may appoint an outside trainer or experienced staff member to coach a new employee in skills relevant to their job but may choose to mentor other staff over a longer term, helping them advance their career.

CASE STUDY

Retaining knowledge at American Express

The management at American Express introduced an initiative in a bid to retain knowledge that could be lost when its workers retired. Those about to retire were invited to shed their responsibilities gradually and spend some of their time teaching and mentoring younger employees. This allowed retiring staff to enjoy the benefits of a salary and workplace engagement for longer, while educating the existing workforce.

94%

of employees would stay longer at a company if it invested in their career

LinkedIn, Workplace Learning Report, 2018

GETTING INVOLVED

There are many ways in which a manager can play an active role in personally mentoring team members:

> **Make time** available.
> **Observe a new team member** as they carry out a task.
> **Informally discuss** how the task went.
> **Invite the team member** to self-evaluate.
> **Offer feedback** and agree on future objectives.
> **Encourage the team member** to try new approaches.

MENTORING

> **Long-term program** in which the manager or another experienced senior staff member (who reports back to the manager) guides one or more employee.
> **Focuses on an individual's** overall professional and personal growth.
> **Sets fluid goals** that can alter as business objectives change.
> **Has an agenda** that evolves over time as the individual develops.

Continuous Learning

A valuable development tool, continuous learning is the practice of ongoing staff training—within and outside of the workplace. Initiated by the manager, it enables personnel to improve their skills and performance and increases their motivation.

Educating employees

Managers can play a critical role in actively facilitating their employees' development at every level, from mentoring within the organization to organizing external courses. An employee will learn on the job through experience, but continuous learning formalizes the process, providing support and resources through an ongoing learning "curve" that yields tangible results. The learning programme should encompass not only job skills, but also include opportunities for intellectual and behavioral growth.

A challenge facing organizations today is that many individuals do not feel they have time to be away from their job to attend courses. As a result, the concept of "learning in the flow of work" has emerged in recent years. Organizations at the forefront of continuous learning now offer digital systems that give employees immediate access to "microlearning" resources, as and when required (see box, right). In any organization, however, managers should seek to nurture the development of the members of their teams by ensuring that they have access to the type of learning programs they most need.

The continuous learning curve

To encourage staff to progress along a curve of continuous learning, managers should provide a range of developmental opportunities. The exact types of training—and the order in which different aspects of learning are undertaken—will vary according to the needs of the individual and the organization.

PERFORMANCE

TIME (YEARS)

CONTINUOUS LEARNING CURVE

DEVELOPMENT CURVE

Initial capability
Assess the skills and attitudes of new starters

Knowledge
Enroll them on formal external courses, as well as in-house training

Continuous professional development
Encourage gaining further qualifications with industry-recognized bodies

Mentoring
Provide employee with access to one-on-one adv and career-path guidance

Collaboration

Allow them to learn new approaches and acquire new tools by working with others

Experience

Facilitate the [ind]ividual's learning [by] giving them new [ta]sks and allowing them to make mistakes

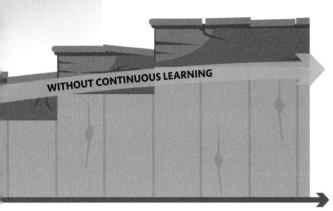

WITHOUT CONTINUOUS LEARNING

MACRO- VS. MICROLEARNING

Most employees have little time for formal expert-led "macrolearning" courses, so self-guided digital "microlearning" tools have become increasingly popular.

Microlearning	Macrolearning
"I need to know now"	"I want to learn new skills"
Requires 5 minutes or less; desk-based	Requires several hours or days; classroom-based
Topic/problem-based	Concepts, principles, and practices
Search the answer to a question	Study exercises set and graded by experts
Personal access to indexed, searchable systems	Learn from experts; get coaching and support
User-friendly, accurate, digital content	Authoritative materials from teacher or author
Sources: videos, articles, microlearning platforms, and workflow learning tools	Sources: courses, classes, and corporate programs

 CASE STUDY

Uber Technologies, Inc.

To help train Uber drivers in Europe, the Middle East, and Sub-Saharan Africa, Uber adopted a microlearning platform via users' smartphones. Drivers who used it were ready to start in the business 13 percent faster than those who attended sessions in person at a training facility. Ongoing training with the learning platform gave drivers more opportunities to earn money and helped increase driver productivity and satisfaction by 8 percent, compared with other drivers.

Performance Management

Managers can gauge the performance of team members by using a performance management system (PMS). This is a framework that defines employees' goals and enables regular discussion of their progress.

Ongoing feedback

A performance management system (PMS) is intended to measure an individual's progress from the day they join an organization, throughout their career, until they leave or retire. By using a PMS, managers can monitor the progress of team members, those team members can receive feedback on their progress, and senior leaders can gain an overall picture of which areas of the organization are thriving and which are not.

Before progress can be measured, the manager sets benchmarks or objectives. These form the starting point of the employee's journey through the company and must be aligned with the values of the organization. Progress should be monitored regularly, while feedback sessions provide an opportunity for managers to give praise and encouragement. At the end of the year, or after an agreed interval, managers should also hold a formal review of the employee's performance.

1. Plan

- **Begin** the process as soon as an employee joins the organization.
- **Agree** on performance expectations and goals with the individual.
- **Make** the objectives time bound by including schedules and deadlines.
- **Ensure** that their goals are consistent with the original job description.
- **Reassess** and reset goals at regular intervals, typically at the start of each business year.

4. Reward

- **Ensure** that the individual's achievements are formally recognized.
- **Provide** a reward in proportion to their achievements and goals. These can include a pay increase; a bonus; a job promotion; time off.
- **Assign** a project specifically tailored to the individual as an opportunity for them to develop further.
- **Ensure** that they are acknowledged by their peers by giving public praise of their achievement.

2. Monitor

> **Measure** performance on a regular basis; conduct reviews no less frequently than monthly or quarterly.
> **Provide** constructive feedback.
> **Coach** the employee to help them reach their performance goals.
> **Adjust** their goals when a change in the business environment forces the organization to reassess its priorities.

The Performance Management system (PMS)

There is no one-size-fits-all PMS—each organization must create a system that reflects its own values and goals. Central to its success is a shared commitment from both managers and employees to strive for goals that are aligned with their organization's objectives. Holding regular monitoring and coaching sessions is helpful for employees and managers alike (see box, right), to encourage continued progression, and prevent bad habits from developing.

CONTINUOUS PERFORMANCE MANAGEMENT

In recent years, organizations such as Adobe and Microsoft have found it productive to treat performance management as an ongoing process in which performance is discussed and reviewed in smaller, consecutive cycles, instead of annually. They have found that more regular performance discussions and more immediate feedback lead to more motivated employees.

AGILE GOALS

REAL-TIME FEEDBACK

DISCUSS DEVELOPMENT

DAILY CHECK-INS

March 10 MONDAY

3. Review

> **Appraise** the employee's performance in a review.
> **Listen** to feedback from peers (including other managers) about the employee.
> **Identify** any adjustments that need to be made to the employee's trajectory.
> **Help** the employee plan their future.

32%
of employees have to wait for more than 3 months to get feedback from their manager

Officevibe survey, 2016

360-degree Feedback

A structured method of assessing an employee's capabilities, 360-degree feedback involves collating views from various coworkers to generate a fair and holistic overview.

Wide-ranging assessment

The first known use of 360-degree feedback was by German military personnel in World War II. Later used by the Esso Research and Engineering Company in the 1950s and General Electric in the 1980s, it is now practiced by a wide variety of organizations.

Feedback on an individual is usually invited from colleagues, the direct supervisor, subordinates, managers of other departments, and even clients or customers. This wide-ranging assessment provides a balanced picture of a person's abilities, compared with one produced by a manager alone.

While the 360-degree technique gives a broad overview of an individual's performance, it is less detailed than a performance appraisal that focuses on specific practical skills and targets. However, managers should give feedback in an objective but positive way; otherwise, the appraisee could be demoralized by any critical comments they receive from respondents.

Subordinates
Team or staff members who report to the appraisee

Structured questionnaire

The 360-degree process involves a structured questionnaire that is used by both the respondents and the appraisee. The questions invite respondents to assess the appraisee in relevant areas such as leadership, teamwork, planning, and achievements. Many organizations now use online questionnaires to help them analyze the information and produce results quickly.

1 Selection
To build trust and confidence, the appraisee should be given as much input as possible into shaping the process. The person may be invited to select the respondents who will rate their performance.

2 Questionnaire
The questionnaire is given to the respondents. The questions should be open-ended and focus on specific skills that the appraisee shows or needs to improve. The appraisee also completes a copy for self-assessment.

3 Results
Results are compiled by the manager, who then discusses them with the appraisee. The feedback is used to help the appraisee build on their strengths and work on areas that need improvement.

Peers
Colleagues of a similar rank to the appraisee

Self
The appraisee, who gives an honest account of themselves

Manager
The appraisee's direct manager or managers

90%
of Fortune 500 companies use 360-degree feedback

Terri Linman, San Diego State University, California, 2006

Customers or clients
People outside the company who depend on the appraisee

✓ NEED TO KNOW

> **Using eight to ten respondents** maximizes the reliability of the feedback results.

> **In some territories**, such as the US, the UK, and the EU, an employee has the right to see information about them held by a company—including any feedback from a 360-degree questionnaire.

COMMUNICATION

Effective Communication

An understanding of the way in which people process visual and written information is the basis of good management. It is fundamental to productive team building, ensuring clarity of purpose and positive connection.

Clear communication

As far back as 1964, subscribers to the *Harvard Business Review* rated the ability to communicate as "the most important factor in making an executive promotable." Numerous reports confirm significant business losses as a result of poor communication.

Good communication skills are vital to every aspect of a manager's role, ensuring they are able to get their points across clearly and concisely when briefing staff, discussing issues, and offering feedback. This also means choosing the right medium (see Communication Tools, pp.176–177) and level of formality and asking the right questions at the right time (see box, far right)—for instance, framing open questions to team members in a straightforward way that is easy to understand.

The ability to listen and respond to staff is another core component, because it motivates and engages others (see Active Listening, pp.170–171). An understanding of nonverbal communication (see pp.172–173) is also important, so that managers do not inadvertently undermine their own messages and are able to interpret accurately others' cues.

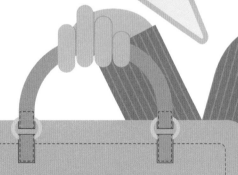

Verbal communication

> **Use short sentences** and simple words for clarity.

> **Speak at an unhurried pace**; allow pauses so that listeners can take in what you say.

> **Hold your head up** and breathe calmly to keep your voice clear.

> **Vary the pitch** and volume of your voice to keep listeners interested.

> **Ask questions** to create dialogue.

Forms of communication

Managers need to be proficient at handling all forms of communication, whether verbal (in person or on the telephone), nonverbal (body language and tone), or written (via letters and emails). Each of these require certain skills to effectively convey meaning and foster a positive personal connection.

Nonverbal communication

> **Make frequent eye contact** (if culturally appropriate) and let facial expressions indicate your interest in the other person.

> **Show respect** for the personal space of others.

> **Dress appropriately** for your environment.

> **Sit or stand straight** to show confidence.

> **Use a warm, pleasant tone of voice** to build rapport.

Assigning tasks effectively

> **Think through your expectations** and frame them clearly, verbally or in writing.

> **Brief the employee directly**; ask them to repeat your instructions to ensure that they understand.

> Discuss with the employee how they plan to carry out the task; check that they have the correct resources.

> **Give a clear deadline** for the task and arrange a follow-up conversation.

QUESTIONS TO AVOID

Open questions invite fuller responses, while some types of questions can alienate staff and should be avoided.

> **Manipulative questions** can sound intimidating and lead to mistrust. Do not say: "So you will send me that summary by tonight, won't you?" Instead, say: "Could you let me have the summary by tonight?"

> **Multiple questions** cause confusion. Do not ask: "When can you do it? How about today? Tomorrow? Or the day after?" Ask a single question only.

> **Destructive questions** can provoke animosity. Do not say: "Are you saying that I am lying?" Instead, find out what the listener is thinking by asking: "What concerns you about what I have just said?"

Written communication

> **Keep your messages concise**; use short words and sentences.

> **Define the main point** or instruction at the start of your message.

> **Use pleasant and respectful** wording, even when raising problems or making criticisms.

> **Close your message** with a clear request for the response or action needed and provide a due date.

> **Proofread your message** before you send it.

> "The art of communication is the language of leadership."
> James Humes, US presidential speechwriter

Active Listening

Active listening means being fully engaged with what a speaker is saying, as well as observing any non-verbal cues. It is an integral part of effective communication, and an essential skill for all managers.

Learning to listen

Research has shown that a manager's performance, and their efficiency as a leader, are directly linked to their ability to listen effectively. This skill is especially important in management, as it has been found that paying attention helps to cultivate a motivated and loyal team—who then have the confidence to share their ideas. Active listening also enables a manager to recall information more accurately and reduces the likelihood of misunderstandings.

Unlike hearing, listening is not an automatic response. Being a proficient listener involves concentrating fully on what the speaker is saying—which is a skill that can be learned and honed over time. Behavioral psychologists also make a distinction between passive and active listening. Passive listening is listening without reacting, whereas active listening requires the listener to respond. This entails picking up on the speaker's body language and tone of voice, mentally taking note of the points that they are making, and resisting the urge to interrupt them.

Mastering the skill of active listening enables managers to open channels of communication within the workplace. Team members are more likely to talk about their ideas or any issues if they feel that they are really being listened to and will perform better as a result.

How to listen actively

Listening with your complete attention encourages the speaker by showing them that they are being heard. An active listener can use nonverbal responses, such as nodding, making eye contact, or smiling—or verbal responses, such as asking relevant questions or recalling particular details. It is important to show active listening thoughout a conversation.

1. Focus
Eliminate distractions by turning off your phone and not trying to multitask; pay attention, be patient, and do not interrupt.

2. Show empathy
Nod to acknowledge the speaker's words, and if fitting, make eye contact.

3. Mirror
Pay attention to the speaker's body language by subtly mirroring it.

4. Paraphrase
Confirm your understanding by repeating in your own words what you believe the speaker has said.

5. Respond
Wait until the speaker has finished talking before you respond to what they have said.

Fewer than
2% of
professionals have had any training in listening skills

Glenn Llopis,
www.forbes.com, 2013

BARRIERS TO ACTIVE LISTENING

> **External distractions**, such as a phone ringing or the noise of traffic on the road outside

> **Physical distractions**, such as thirst, hunger, a headache, or the need to go to the bathroom

> **Internal distractions**, such as thinking about how to respond before the speaker has finished

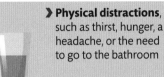
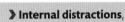

Nonverbal Communication

The messages people convey through nonverbal signals are often more revealing than their words. Understanding their meaning can help managers interact better with their colleagues, staff, and clients.

A powerful tool

People's facial expressions and gestures can powerfully influence their interactions with those around them. Research into this area of study—kinesics—was pioneered by anthropologist Ray Birdwhistell, first outlined in his book *Introduction to Kinesics* (1952). It reveals that 55 percent of communication is body language, 38 percent is vocal (such as tone of voice), and only 7 percent is verbal.

Effective use of nonverbal cues can influence workplace outcomes. For instance, a manager who smiles, uses a light tone, and has a relaxed posture when giving feedback to staff can create a positive impression, even when difficult subjects are being broached. However, unwitting use of negative body language may have an adverse effect. A stiff posture and avoidance of eye contact when meeting a new client could be interpreted as hostility, and neutral feedback delivered with negative body language can be viewed as criticism.

CHECK YOUR APPEARANCE

The way you dress creates a first impression. Ensure that your clothing and grooming are appropriate for your audience, your reasons for communicating, and the setting.

CONTAIN YOUR MOVEMENTS

When making gestures, keep them small and close to your body because this gives an image of confidence and authority. A low but audible voice and a relaxed posture add to a sense of calm control.

Using nonverbal cues

In the workplace and elsewhere, gestures, tone, eye contact, and posture can instantly convey a message over and above your words. Being aware of your own body language and that of others, and understanding what it indicates, can prove invaluable in interactions with colleagues and in negotiations.

SAME GESTURE, DIFFERENT MEANING

Not all the members of a global organization may read body language the same way. Some gestures can have quite different connotations in different cultures. For instance, enthusiastic arm gestures are thought impolite in Japan, and a thumbs-up can be considered a rude sign in certain Islamic countries (see pp.28–29).

93% of communication is nonverbal

Ray Birdwhistell,
Introduction to Kinesics, 1952

BE CAUTIOUS WITH TOUCH

The expectations or prohibitions on touching others in a business context vary from culture to culture. Managers should make sure they are aware of and respect local customs.

BE AWARE OF EYE CONTACT

Making eye contact with someone usually reinforces trust; however, in some Asian cultures, looking a superior in the eye as you speak can be considered a disrespectful action.

USE VOCAL DYNAMICS

How something is said can be more important than what is said. Tone, volume, rate, pitch, forcefulness, and enunciation all contribute to the meaning of the words that are used and convey how the speaker feels about the people in the room.

ELECTRONIC COMMUNICATION MODES

With ever-advancing technology, and as businesses pursue global connectivity and instant access to information, fewer transactions are conducted face to face, and other forms of communication are used instead (see pp.176–177). In the absence of body language, it is crucial to avoid misunderstanding. Here are a few guidelines for phone calls, emails, and instant messaging.

 Phone calls
A short, sharp tone can sound frustrated or even angry when the listener can not see your facial expression. Using a light, cheery voice on the phone conveys friendliness.

 Email
Phrases such as "Kind regards" are a sign of politeness and respect. Avoid more officious ones, such as "per my last email," which can sound rude or condescending.

 Instant messaging
In informal correspondence, an emoji such as a smiley face can help convey the intent and context of your message. But be careful not to use emojis that contradict some other part of the message, because they can seem snide.

Giving Feedback

Every organization relies on its personnel to perform their roles effectively and work toward common goals. Giving and receiving feedback on performance is a key part of this process.

Making feedback work

It is widely recognized that when it is constructive and communicated well, feedback—whether from team leaders to team members or from staff to management—benefits organizational efficiency (see pp.164–165). Feedback can occur informally on a daily basis, but it is also an important part of a formal and structured appraisal process. Crucial to an employee's feeling of being valued, it can also provide a sense of progression that can be more motivating than other incentive-based factors, such as a pay increase.

How managers give feedback can influence whether staff make progress or become demoralized. Research by the Center for Creative Leadership has shown that unconstructive, harshly delivered feedback is ineffective, as it may cause the recipient to feel defensive, while feedback—whether positive or negative—delivered in a constructive manner is crucial for staff development. However, a manager's focus should not be only on a person's strengths. Ignoring weaknesses gives a false impression to the recipient and obstructs the improvement of teamwork. Instead, managers should deliver any negative feedback in a constructive, nonjudgemental way.

Allow the recipient an opportunity to give feedback on how well they feel they are managed to help open a two-way dialogue.

Give feedback promptly, otherwise, team members may feel frustrated that they were left to continue their tasks without due correction.

Strategies for delivering feedback

Managers should give prompt feedback that is specific but not personal and ensure it is delivered positively—both in terms of wording and emotional signals (see box, right). Questions should be kept open-ended, allowing the recipient to develop their own thoughts in response.

Deliver feedback positively and constructively. Framing feedback negatively can feel threatening for the recipient.

Ask questions to stimulate reflection instead of lecturing the recipient. Encouraging self-reflection could help the recipient experiment with different ideas and explore new approaches.

EMOTIONAL SIGNALS

Business professor at the University of Miami Marie Dasborough studied two groups of people receiving feedback. The first group was given negative feedback accompanied by positive emotional signals, such as smiles and nods. The second group received positive feedback accompanied by negative emotional signals, for example, frowning and a critical gaze. In follow-up interviews, those in the first group felt better about their performance than those in the second group. In other words, the way in which feedback is delivered can have a more powerful motivational effect than the content itself.

Ensure that feedback is not personal. Whether positive or negative, your comments should relate to a person's performance in their role, and not to their character.

Be specific rather than general. Feedback should focus on particular examples of a behavior, noting the time and place.

40%
of workers are actively disengaged when they get little or no feedback

Forbes, 2017

Communication Tools

When face-to-face communication is not possible, it is important to choose the correct alternative method, which depends on the audience, the context, and the nature of the message.

Virtually face to face

Communications theorist Marshall McLuhan coined the phrase "the medium is the message" in 1964, which means that the way a message is understood depends on how it is delivered. This idea still underpins approaches to communication today.

Although conventional tools such as phone and email remain mainstays of communication, managers are increasingly turning to more sophisticated cloud-based software and platforms that enable remote communication via apps. Similar to social media, these platforms allow team members to work as if they are in a virtual meeting room that is always open, using group chats or video conferencing, sharing documents, and creating work. Being able to talk to employees in this way reduces the need for travel, and managers can monitor their team's workflow and contribute from almost anywhere.

Types of tools

There are two main groups of communication tools: one-way and two-way. One-way tools are effectively bulletin boards, but they can reach a large audience and so are good for informing or educating staff. For immediate feedback or training, however, two-way tools are more suitable.

One-way

Intranet
An intranet (internal network of computers) is a useful way of getting a message across to large numbers of employees.

Webcasts
These are good for educating employees—presentations and events are broadcast live over the internet.

Webinars
Like webcasts, webinars (web seminars) are useful teaching tools. Some include limited audience participation.

Two-way

Email
This has replaced postal mail in many instances and is a rapid way to keep in touch with colleagues and customers alike.

Web conferences
A web conference enables people in different locations to participate in a meeting and share documents.

Telephone
A telephone call or conversation via text message allows two or more people to communicate instantly.

By using social collaboration tools, companies can increase worker productivity by

25%

McKinsey Global Institute, 2012

TOP TOOLS: WHICH ONE WHEN?

When	Which tool
Employees do not know who to contact if they have questions or need details of members within departments and who they report to	**Company intranet** with employee profiles
Managers lose track of project progress dates and deadlines or projects stall while awaiting approval from senior management	**Workflow tool** with progress steps, notifications, and alerts
Staff miss vital information sent via email, and managers are unsure if emails were received	**Alerts** and notifications tool
Customer retention is declining, customer feedback is negative, or employees are missing customer or interdepartmental queries	**Issue-tracking** software

Podcasts
Information concerning a project or a change in company policy can be uploaded to the internet as a digital audio file.

Presentations
A presentation, whether live or recorded, is an excellent way to convey vital information to a large audience.

Voicemail
In emergencies or when the internet is down, messages can be left on employees' voicemail.

Video-sharing sites
Sites such as YouTube enable users to view or upload videos, which may be instructional, on almost any topic.

Collaborative platforms
Web-based platforms such as Sharepoint enable team members to chat, share files, and work together on projects.

Communication apps
Apps such as Slack and Flock offer collaboration services ranging from video conferencing to task tracking.

Issue-tracking software
This software tracks communication history, aiding accountability and helping resolve issues promptly.

Effective Meetings

Meetings facilitate communication, collaboration, and decision-making. By following some simple guidelines, managers can ensure that meetings are well executed and boost their teams' performance.

Enhancing effectiveness

Meetings are essential in any organization and are an integral part of management. In their simplest form, they are a way for managers to share information with their staff, peers, or seniors, such as routine team updates. Such meetings can be informal and do not need an agenda or for minutes to be taken. The manager should relay the information clearly, using handouts or slides as required, then invite questions to make sure everyone has understood.

In contrast, meetings at which decisions are required, such as agreeing to a plan, must be structured. To be effective, an agenda should be set and followed. Although the manager may lead the meeting, they should encourage others to participate and actively listen. Minutes must be taken, recording what was said by whom, what has been discussed, and any decisions made. These should then be circulated after the meeting to all participants and used to follow up on any outcomes agreed.

Types of meetings

When calling a meeting, managers must decide what type of meeting it will be and clearly communicate its purpose to attendees. Setting an appropriate venue and time slot is also vital—shorter for updates and information-sharing meetings, longer for brainstorming or problem-solving meetings. Managers should also be clear on their role in the meeting, from chairing, delegating, or sharing information to encouraging creativity.

Regular status updates

These allow the manager to share information or request it from their team members. Meetings can be quick and informal.

Information-sharing

To be effective, the manager must have all the information required and be willing and able to answer questions from attendees.

Decision-making

Although a manager may lead the meeting, the participation of all attendees should be encouraged in order to reach agreements.

MAKING MEETINGS WORTHWHILE

Studies have shown that poorly prepared meetings can be unproductive and waste participants' time. To maximize the productivity of meetings, achieve tangible results, and leave participants feeling that their time has been well spent, managers should consider the following factors, dependent on the type of meeting:

 》 Decide on the objective of the meeting and make sure all participants fully understand it so that they can decide whether they need to attend.

 》 Provide an agenda ahead of time, so that attendees can bring all necessary information with them or prepare questions.

 》 Limit the duration of the meeting to the time necessary to meet its aims. Do not arrange a 60-minute meeting if only 45 minutes is required.

 》 Soon after the meeting, produce minutes (having first invited a good minute taker). These should list decisions and time frames for actions.

 》 Follow up with participants to ensure that all actions are being executed in accordance with the minutes.

75%
of workers receive
no formal training
in how to conduct meetings
TED.com, 2017

Problem-solving
Depending on the problem, informal brainstorming sessions, (see pp.156–157) facilitated by the manager, can be very productive.

Innovating
Similar to problem-solving meetings; the manager should welcome all ideas and allow the attendees to discuss their merits.

Ideas-sharing
Most productive when people are relaxed; the manager should allow everyone to speak freely and bounce ideas off each other.

Presentations

Being able to engage an audience and convey a core message with a persuasive presentation is a key managerial skill. However, preparing and delivering good presentations takes practice.

Grabbing attention

The best presentations are often those that rely on graphics more than words. When Steve Jobs made presentations for Apple, the audience took notice – not just because of who he was, but also because his delivery had impact. Analysts point to his technique of often just presenting a large statistic or number on a slide, with minimal text to qualify it. This simple, graphic-centered approach—one number/fact per slide—is now the standard presentation method for all Apple executives, and it is a good example for managers to follow.

It is important to fully research the audience beforehand so they can be engaged with a presentation they can relate to. This enables the presenter to appeal to people's needs by including stories, figures, and facts that will be relevant to them. When putting a presentation together, consideration should be given to audience members who have difficulty hearing or reading.

Preparation is crucial – not only for working out what to say and creating slides, but also for anticipating possible questions.

Presenting well

An effective presentation is one that the audience will remember. Making regular eye contact with attendees, smiling, and using open, natural gestures all help make a speaker appear more competent. Learning to speak in public with passion and conviction, and to answer questions confidently, will earn any manager the respect of their audience.

1 Prepare

Find out who will be coming and tailor the content accordingly. Send an agenda in advance to remind people to attend.

2 Make slides creative

Vary the template and colors of slides and include images to help get the message across. Use easy-to-read fonts: a point size of 30 works well.

5 Stimulate the audience

Keep the audience focused by asking rhetorical questions, citing research and anecdotes from experience, and quoting experts.

6 Close

End the presentation by summarizing its key points, calling for action if required, and asking the audience for questions.

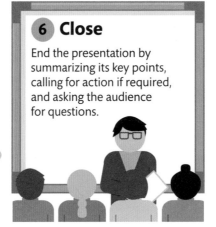

7 Question ready

Develop your own questions (in case no one asks), research widely to prepare for a variety of questions, and have useful facts and figures on hand.

FONTS FOR PRESENTATIONS

The ideal presentation font has excellent legibility, especially at a distance, and conveys an image in keeping with the topic. Here are six to consider as alternatives to Calibri, the standard font for Microsoft PowerPoint:

Franklin Gothic: strong, approachable; many weights and widths available

Garamond: elegant, sophisticated; good for small print

Segoe UI: extensive range of symbols; good for headings and small print

Tahoma: clear, distinct characters; suited to scientific or technical text

Impact: dramatic, heavy; ideal for strong headings

Verdana: developed for legibility on screens; good for small text

CASE STUDY

The "Ratner effect"

On April 23, 1991, successful jewelry entrepreneur Gerald Ratner made a speech that effectively destroyed the multimillion-pound empire that he had built up from his father's modest retail business. In front of an audience consisting of more than 6,000 business people and journalists, Ratner made a statement that became his undoing—raising the question of whether he was unprepared or was simply trying to be amusing. When asked how his stores could sell a sherry decanter for just £4.95, he replied "... because it's total crap." Consequently, the value of the company's shares fell by £500 million in a few days, and Ratner lost both the business and his personal wealth, which was tied up in shares.

3 Open with impact

Connect emotionally as well as intellectually with the audience by starting with a humorous or touching story or a startling fact.

4 Explain the objective of the presentation

Introduce each idea separately, one point per slide, and back up each point with a statistic.

> "People who know what they're talking about don't need PowerPoint."

Steve Jobs, Co-founder of Apple Inc.

8 Final close

Bring the audience's attention back to the goal by reiterating the key points and calling for action again if relevant.

9 Follow-up

Keep up the momentum of the presentation by emailing a summary to attendees and asking for feedback to improve future presentations.

✓ NEED TO KNOW

> **The core message** is the key point of a presentation. It needs to be communicated clearly and briefly.

> **Nonverbal communication** (see pp.172–173) is the practice of using gestures and body language to help get a message across. Speakers should use open, confident gestures and move around when presenting to help keep the audience engaged.

Corporate Communications

Corporate communications is the practice of developing an organization's reputation and conveying its values to an internal and external audience. Having a good reputation is fundamental to the success of a company.

Sending the right message

Most organizations have an individual, team, or department that is responsible for corporate communications. This role involves managing the organization's image and reputation and promoting its values both internally to employees and externally to media and stakeholders (including shareholders, partners, customers, and clients).

In its infancy, corporate communications focused on company products and so specialized in setting up external publicity events and writing press releases. More recently, the focus has shifted toward cultivating staff engagement and fostering employee well-being. This has led to organizations setting up intranets to share information and holding regular meetings with employees to discuss performance and future goals. However, the key task of corporate communications remains to manage an organization's reputation, since any change in this can have an effect on revenue, workplace productivity, and employee retention.

INTERNAL COMMUNICATION

Employee well-being

> **Develop an intranet** for sharing company information and keeping staff engaged

> **Provide forums for employees** to share and give feedback

> **Involve frontline managers** to communicate company goals to employees at all levels

> **Publish employment policies online**, enabling stakeholders to see how the organization is implementing its employee well-being program

> **Manage change** by sharing information with staff as soon as it is available; take regular surveys on how the organization is responding to the change; celebrate milestone goals with progress parties

Companies with effective internal communications offer

47%

higher returns for shareholders

Towers Watson, professional services firm, 2010

Cementing a reputation

The overall goal of a corporate communications manager is to build an organization's reputation—as an employer who people want to work for and as a responsible contributor to the community. Both internal and external communications are vital in creating and maintaining this image.

EXTERNAL COMMUNICATION

Media relations

❯ **Be honest and open** in media communications. Stay true to organizational values and ensure that words are supported by actions

Social responsibility

❯ **Take a stand on social issues**—this will improve employee engagement and promote the organization's image

❯ **Send out a clear, convincing message** to show how the company is taking action on these social issues (stakeholders will reject messages that seem hollow)

❯ **Time the delivery of a message well**; speaking out too soon on an issue can seem rushed, and any message needs to be carefully thought out

Sustainability

❯ **Announce sustainability goals**, then measure progress

❯ **Report this progress to employees and stakeholders**, who will be influenced by the organization's standing in the community

Corporate philanthropy

❯ **Use social media to promote organizational philanthropy**—for example, fundraising events

❯ **Present data in the form of infographics** to convey philanthropic causes and effects in an appealing, accessible way

Reputation

❯ **Show the organization** to be a good employer

❯ **Promote the organization's efforts** to be an ethical business

CASE STUDY

Marks & Spencer

Underlining the importance of organizations conveying integrity, British retailer Marks & Spencer faced a backlash in 2019 from the media and consumers after a giveaway promotion aimed at children that offered single-use plastic toys. The campaign was at odds with the company's publicized corporate policy of cutting out plastic packaging and achieving zero waste by 2025.

COMMUNICATING EFFECTIVELY

Goals for communications managers include:

❯ **Keep employees engaged:** help employees cope with organizational change and understand how the company's goals are relevant to them.

❯ **Plan internal and external communications carefully:** create more interesting content, adapt content produced by others, and identify stakeholders who can help deliver a key message.

❯ **Rethink digital communication:** try a variety of technologies, such as apps or social media, to establish which channel is most likely to reach the target audience.

Crisis Communications

In business terms, a crisis is a situation that can harm an organization or threaten its clients or customers. In such situations, managers need a plan of action.

Being prepared

Some crises will be internal, such as when a company's assets lose value or the company cannot afford to pay its debt; others will be external, such as when a product is found to be harmful to consumers. The dangers arise not just from the situation itself but from the effect it has on an organization's public profile.

Even an internal crisis can quickly develop into an external crisis if the issue reaches social media or traditional news channels. For this reason, managers need to anticipate possible crises and develop a plan to deal with them. Prompt, clear communication, both within the organization and with outside parties, can make the difference between recovery and disaster.

The initial response should be immediate, acknowledging what has happened and showing compassion for those affected. This should be followed by an announcement between 24 and 48 hours later, stating the key facts. Managers need time to gather information, but public unrest will grow if they wait too long. At such times, legal support may be needed, but this should be handled carefully; it must be seen to benefit those affected by the crisis rather than merely protect the organization.

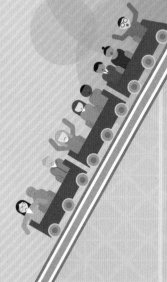

1. Identify potential risks to the organization or brand and assess how likely they are to occur.

2. Make a list of stakeholders— those who need to be kept informed in the event of a crisis, including managers and employees, clients, investors, media outlets, and the general public.

3. Anticipate potential data breach crises by creating data-breach platforms and emergency websites that can be activated if a breach happens.

4. Set out communications guidelines by appointing a spokesperson to represent or speak for the company. Define what information should be conveyed—and when and where.

5. Ensure that the plan covers all areas of the organization and not just communications.

6. Test the plan by carrying out training and practice runs so that the crisis-management team (made up of senior managers, spokespersons, and legal and PR experts) is prepared.

Precrisis: prepare crisis plan

7. Monitor all media forms, looking for any fluctuations or inconsistencies in the way in which the organization's business is being reported.

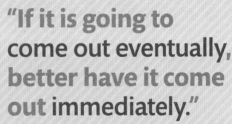

"If it is going to come out eventually, better have it come out immediately."

Henry Kissinger, former US Secretary of State, 1982

8. Activate emergency communications as soon as a crisis occurs so that the spokesperson can give an immediate response.

60% of board members say that it took over a year for their organization to recover from a crisis

"A Crisis of Confidence," Deloitte, 2016

9. Between 24 and 48 hours later, ensure that the spokesperson conveys key facts to stakeholders, staff, and the media. Provide a schedule of further announcements and follow this up with regular updates.

10. Establish virtual and physical communications centers to handle inquiries and deal with website, social media, and customer service questions.

11. If necessary, seek advice from legal advisors, a PR agency, or subject matter experts.

12. Analyze the crisis once it is under control. Determine how effective the plan was and what could be done to improve it in the future.

Acute crisis: activate crisis plan   **Postcrisis**

Persuasion and Influence

Being skilled in the art of positive persuasion is a great asset in people-management and the key to successful negotiation. The more persuasive a manager is, the greater their influence in the workplace.

Nurturing positivity

Persuasion is more effective at eliciting change than compulsion—imposing decisions rarely earns respect or motivates. But persuasion is time-consuming, so it is worth assessing in advance who can be persuaded, and how. The manager must define the issue to be addressed, but involving staff in discussions will make them feel that they are being treated fairly and that their views are being listened to. While persuading those with opposing views may be the main aim, existing supporters should not be ignored: support evaporates quickly when people are taken for granted. It may be best initially to look for short-term change. Getting a "foot in the door"—gaining a small commitment now—can start a process that leads to greater changes in the long term. And it is not always necessary to persuade everyone at once. Since people are affected by the attitudes of their peers, obtaining the support of a few at first can trigger a ripple effect, leading to wider acceptance later on.

Creating synergy

Accomplished persuaders leave people feeling better off, however brief the interaction, and they have this effect not only in face-to-face and small-group encounters, but also when addressing broader segments of the organization. Sincerity and empathy are essential—being perceived as trustworthy and credible will increase a manager's influence. Appealing to the common good, using "we" rather than "I", helps others to identify with your viewpoint, and reminding listeners that they are free to make their own decisions shows respect. Conversely, scare tactics create an unhelpful climate of fear, while constant nagging (a common sign of micromanagement) causes people to disengage.

Being persuasive
> **Choose the right time and place** to make the argument. Practice your pitch to avoid seeming uncertain.

> **Make simple, logical points**; eliminate negatives and emphasize positives.

PRACTICING PERSUASION

Ancient Greek philosopher Aristotle outlined four modes of persuasion that can be utilized by managers to ensure their proposals have the strongest chance of success.

❯ **Ethos (character)**: making sure that you are qualified to make your argument, having gained the relevant expertise through experience

❯ **Pathos (feeling)**: using passion, imagination, and vision to appeal to your listeners' emotions

❯ **Logos (word)**: presenting your message clearly and logically, having researched the details of your proposed course of action

❯ **Kairos (opportune moment)**: choosing the best opportunity for communicating your message and ensuring that it is tailored to your audience

"The greatest ability in business is to get along with others and to influence their actions."

John Hancock, US merchant and statesman, c.1776

❯ **Explain the benefits** and personal advantages to your listeners.

❯ **If your audience is initially sceptical**, opposing arguments can be neutralized by raising them yourself in a mild form and then refuting them.

Exerting influence

❯ **Nurture relationships**, whether with team members, service users, customers, or stakeholders.

❯ **Be likeable** and curtail any annoying behaviors or habits.

❯ **Build trust** and establish credibility by honoring promises and commitments and being consistent.

❯ **Display empathy** and demonstrate an understanding of other people's perspectives.

Negotiation

Negotiation can be a minefield, but managers who become skilled at it are highly valued. To succeed, all types of negotiation require thorough preparation and clear, unambiguous communication.

Realistic objectives

The role of a manager frequently involves negotiation. This can take place between organizations, between different departments of a single organization, and between teams. Not all negotiations are successful, but careful planning increases the likelihood of a positive outcome.

First, a negotiator must set realistic objectives—in line with organizational goals rather than personal ones—and decide on the minimum acceptable outcome. Secondly, they should research the other party and assess their likely interests. That way, when the other party puts forward their position, the negotiator is then equipped to question and respond effectively. They can perhaps probe the other party's interests further to discover their true motivation or reply with a counterposition that the other party will consider more acceptable.

Negotiation can take place by email or phone or face to face (either online or in person). The overall style of the negotiation, whether assertive, passive, or aggressive, should be carefully considered (see box, right). The choices made during the communication will determine its success or failure. At any stage, the negotiator can concede, make polite demands, threaten, or, if the negotiation stalls, suggest a further joint discussion.

A three-step strategy

The negotiation process is a little like a duel. It is best to prepare well, assessing your opponent's strengths and thinking through your tactics; you do not want to be caught off guard. When you meet, an initial charm offensive before you set out your position can be disarming. Finally, guided by your opponent's reactions, close a deal or agree on the next steps.

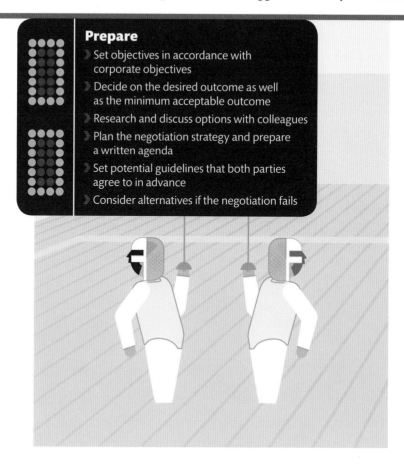

Prepare

- Set objectives in accordance with corporate objectives
- Decide on the desired outcome as well as the minimum acceptable outcome
- Research and discuss options with colleagues
- Plan the negotiation strategy and prepare a written agenda
- Set potential guidelines that both parties agree to in advance
- Consider alternatives if the negotiation fails

NEGOTIATION STYLE

To negotiate successfully, it is important to cultivate the correct manner, both of speech and body language (see pp.172–173). The goal is to be assertive and to avoid the extremes of being passive or aggressive.

Passive
> Submissive
> Noncommittal
> Emotional and defensive
> Uses ambiguous language

Assertive
> Confident
> Steady
> Factual rather than emotional
> Makes statements starting with "I"

Aggressive
> Confrontational
> Hostile
> Blames the other party
> Makes statements starting with "You"

NEED TO KNOW

> **The BPA** is the best possible agreement—the one that meets the negotiator's and the other party's interests.
> **The ZOPA** is the zone of possible agreement—the range of options that each party would accept.
> **The BATNA** is the best alternative to a negotiated agreement—in other words, plan B.
> **The bottom line** is the point beyond which neither negotiator will proceed because it is not in their interests to do so.

Engage

> Introduce yourself and build a rapport
> Ask questions to probe the other party's interests (their needs and motivations)
> Make your offer and listen to their response; a first offer is rarely accepted. All proposals should be seen as legitimate and fair
> Consider compromises; seek concessions; make concessions
> Create value by offering options: conditions, contingencies, and trade-offs

Close
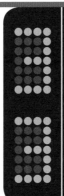
> Observe physical signals from the other party: are they looking tired? Are their arguments fading?
> Summarize agreements and concessions
> Get agreements in writing
> Follow up on agreed commitments
> Suggest mediation, or a second discussion, if agreement cannot be reached
> Be prepared to walk away

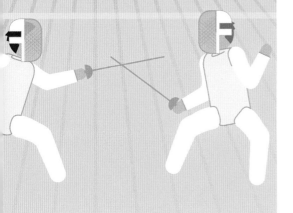
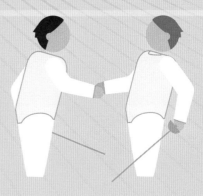

Resolving Disputes

A dispute can be difficult to resolve, especially when parties are entrenched in their positions. It falls to the manager to find a fair, appropriate solution that minimizes disruption to the organization.

The peace process

A manager who has to settle a dispute—in the workplace or with a client—must remain detached, act quickly, listen empathetically, and work toward a practical solution step by step. To achieve this, it helps to know the best approach to adopt in a particular situation. In 1974, US academics Kenneth Thomas and Ralph Kilmann published their research on the subject in their bestselling book *The Thomas-Kilmann Conflict Mode Instrument*. The book sets out five styles for resolving conflict, each using a different balance of assertiveness and cooperation.

Resolving any type of dispute, or mediating between two parties, usually requires a difficult conversation with one or both sides. Being prepared for it—armed with all the relevant information and knowing each party's legal rights—is crucial. Conducting the conversation in an appropriate, unhurried way—

and with empathy—can diffuse a heated situation and partially improve working relationships.

Start conversations as soon as possible after a problem arises, but only once all parties have calmed down. If the issue is a workplace conflict, it may be best to set up a

regular meeting to allow grievances to be aired and dealt with before they become disputes (see pp.152–153). Following any dispute (internal or external), any resolutions should be set in writing and communicated to everyone involved.

Five strategies for resolving differences

Kenneth Thomas and Ralph Kilmann propose five approaches for diffusing conflict and bringing it to an end. The Thomas-Kilmann Conflict Mode Instrument uses a matrix that measures levels of assertiveness on one axis and cooperation on the other. A manager must decide the most appropriate approach to take.

ASSERTIVENESS

ASSERTIVE

UNASSERTIVE

UNCOOPERATIVE

Competing

> Each party pursues their own concerns, regardless of the impact on the other.

> This method is assertive and uncooperative; each party uses whatever power they feel is necessary to win.

> Appropriate if defending a situation believed to be correct, either morally or legally.

Avoiding

> Both parties avoid confrontation; they pursue neither their own concerns nor those of the other person.

> This style is both unassertive and uncooperative.

> Appropriate if attempting diplomatically to sidestep an issue, postpone it until a more appropriate time, or withdraw from a threatening situation.

FUNCTIONAL AND DYSFUNCTIONAL CONFLICT

Not all workplace disagreements are bad. A certain amount of conflict is healthy, but it depends on the type.

Functional conflict is positive and leads to constructive criticism and healthy debate about issues, such as how much money to invest and the organization's direction.

Dysfunctional conflict, such as defamatory remarks or withholding information to gain power, is negative. It can cause tension among team members and lead to increased stress and low levels of employee satisfaction.

54%
of employees believe that managers could handle disputes more effectively

Workplace Conflict and How Businesses Can Harness It to Thrive,
CPP Global Human Capital Report, 2008

Collaborating

❯ Parties work together to resolve a dispute in a way that satisfies them both.

❯ Method is assertive and cooperative—the exact opposite of "Avoiding."

❯ Appropriate when parties want to fully explore a disagreement and learn from each other's insights to find a creative solution.

Compromising

❯ Both parties try to find the middle ground to "split" their differences— a win-win outcome.

❯ Moderately assertive and moderately cooperative.

❯ Appropriate when the objective is a solution to satisfy both parties; it addresses an issue more than "Avoiding" but not in as much depth as "Collaborating."

Accommodating

❯ One party sacrifices their own self-interest to satisfy the other.

❯ Unassertive and highly cooperative—the exact opposite of "Competing."

❯ Appropriate if the other party needs help or is right or if one party wants to demonstrate goodwill and maintain positive relationships for the future.

COOPERATIVE

LEVEL OF COOPERATION

SELF-MANAGEMENT

Time Management

Time is a valuable, finite resource that must be used wisely to achieve success. Managers can use a range of methods to ensure that their time—and that of any team member—is used effectively.

Using time wisely

For managers, the key to effective time management is to understand how time is being spent. Keeping a log over a period of days or weeks is a good starting point and helps highlight any anomalies. The next step is to analyze the activities recorded in the log to evaluate how they compare to organizational priorities. If identifying potential collaborations with similar organizations is a key objective, and only 10 percent of time is spent on cultivating links with prospective partners, the reasons for this should be explored.

The next thing to do is to plan, focusing attention on key tasks and the amount of time that each ideally requires. It is important that tasks are prioritized objectively and that time estimates are not overoptimistic, since it can be demotivating if plans are not realized. It is helpful to categorize tasks according to importance and urgency. For example, restoring telephone and IT services in a country hotel is likely to be both

The Pareto principle

Named after Italian economist Vilfredo Pareto, the Pareto principle is the observation that for any given activity, roughly 80 percent of output comes from 20 percent of inputs. From a managerial perspective, this means that 80 percent of the effort spent on a project could potentially be wasted. And so it is vital that managers identify the most productive 20 percent of their activities and give them the highest priority.

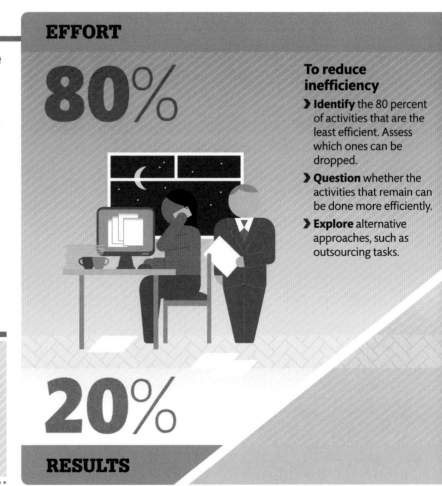

EFFORT

80%

20%

RESULTS

To reduce inefficiency

❯ **Identify** the 80 percent of activities that are the least efficient. Assess which ones can be dropped.

❯ **Question** whether the activities that remain can be done more efficiently.

❯ **Explore** alternative approaches, such as outsourcing tasks.

✓ NEED TO KNOW

❯ **Parkinson's Law**, published in *The Economist* in 1955, states that "work is elastic in its time"—it can stretch (or be compressed) to fill its allotted time.

urgent and important, whereas analyzing guest surveys for the monthly review meeting is important but not urgent. Planning in this way helps determine which activities should be completed first.

Lastly, managers can create an environment that is conducive to good time management. For example, personnel might be encouraged to adopt techniques such as structuring their day according to their times of peak productivity and to break down complex projects into smaller tasks.

"**Most people get ahead during the** time **that other people waste.**"

Henry Ford, founder of the Ford Motor Company

EFFECTIVENESS AND EFFICIENCY

Two concepts that are often confused with each other are effectiveness and efficiency. Being effective is about working to achieve the right goals—those that deliver the desired results. For a manager, this means ensuring that their team is correctly focused. In contrast, being efficient means making the best use of one's resources to achieve one's goals, such as manufacturing a product with the minimum amount of waste and at the lowest possible cost. As such, efficiency is an ongoing state of improvement that a manager may encourage from their team once its effectiveness has been established.

EFFORT
20%

To maximize efficiency

❭ **Identify** the 20 percent of activities that are the most efficient. Assess what factors make them successful.

❭ **Explore** whether any of the identified measures can be applied to the less productive activities.

❭ **Prioritize** the small number of activities that produce more.

80%
RESULTS

Being effective means identifying and hitting the correct target.

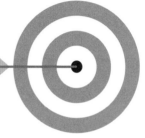

Being efficient means hitting the target without wasted effort.

ersonal Imp ct

Understanding and developing your personal impact will help you to create effective relationships and build a successful career.

Being self-aware

Personal impact relates to the effect that a person has on others, and how they and their ideas are received. Studies have shown that we form an opinion of a person within a second of meeting them—but our opinions are often mistaken. All kinds of unconscious biases affect our judgment, based on anything from their body language to their clothing.

The way to overcome these biases is to develop self-awareness. This involves becoming mindful of our responses to others and, crucially, of other people's responses to us. The latter is particularly important, since other people have biases, too. For example, if an interviewee believes that managers in general are rude and overbearing, this may affect how they approach an interview, regardless of the interviewer's manner.

Personal impact can also affect success in the workplace. If a manager is too dominant, people may be reluctant to venture their opinions, and new ideas may be missed. Likewise, if someone is perceived as being weak, others may ignore them, and their voice remains unheard.

The Johari window

One way of increasing self-awareness is by using the Johari window technique. Developed by US psychologists Joseph Luft and Harrington Ingham, it gives people a clearer view of who they are. As such, it is an invaluable tool for managers and employees alike (see below).

Learning to be open

The Johari window divides the personality into four quadrants: aspects that are known both to us and to others; aspects that are known to us but not others; aspects that are known to others but not us; and aspects that are known to neither us nor others. To achieve greater self-understanding, it is important to compare how we see ourselves to how we are seen by others. The goal is to increase the size of the first quadrant of the window—our "open self"—by seeking feedback and revealing more about ourselves.

The "open self"
Aspects of yourself that both you and others know (e.g., that you are outgoing, friendly, and like to be with others)

The "hidden self"
Aspects of yoursel that you know bu others do not kno (e.g., that you ar obsessed with fitne

1

Resolve
To improve your relationships, resolve to expand the scope of your open self.

MANAGING EMOTIONS

US writer Daniel Goleman drew on the ideas of US psychologists Peter Salovey and John Mayer to write *Emotional Intelligence* (1998). Unlike IQ, which relates to cognitive intelligence, emotional intelligence or EQ involves understanding our emotions, the emotions of others, and how we communicate feelings. There are five dimensions:

> **Self-awareness**: the ability to recognize moods and emotions
> **Self-regulation**: the ability to recover from setbacks and to manage disruptive moods
> **Motivation**: the ability to achieve goals for personal reasons, without external rewards
> **Empathy**: the ability to understand the emotions of other people
> **Social relationships**: the ability to form networks and build rapport

The "blind self"
Aspects of yourself that others know but you do not know (e.g., that you are a calming presence)

The "unknown self"
Aspects of yourself that neither you nor others know (perhaps that you are resilient or exceptionally brave)

"**Knowing** others is intelligence; **knowing** yourself is true wisdom."

Lao Tzu, Chinese philosopher, 6th century BCE

2

Learn
Discover things that others know about you but you do not by seeking feedback.

3

Inform
Help others understand you better by revealing more about yourself.

4

Be aware
Understand that there are things about you that both you and others have yet to discover.

Building a Career

Achieving a successful career in management takes time and effort. It involves understanding yourself, setting and assessing personal goals, and recognizing opportunities to progress.

Setting objectives

Effective management involves leading others, making decisions, and taking responsibility—it can also mean working under pressure. For anyone considering a career in management, the first step is to question whether they have the skills and personality it requires. Existing managers looking to progress should also assess their strengths in these areas, then decide whether their skills and ideas are current and whether they really would thrive in a more demanding role.

In order to develop a management career, it is important to set objectives. Although the route taken will always reflect the opportunities that arise, aspiring to chairmanship will be a different journey to that of team leader.

> ## "Management is efficiency in climbing the ladder of success."
>
> Stephen Covey, *The 7 Habits of Highly Effective People*, 1989

4

ACTIVELY SEEK OPPORTUNITIES

Practice new skills—for example, by volunteering to give a presentation. Be visible in the organization. Talk to people who may help with career development.

Planning and managing a career

While certain jobs offer structured progression, most people's careers develop organically, with upward or lateral moves—and sometimes downward ones. There is no set path to follow: the route will depend on the individual, the field of work, and the openings available. However, people can take certain steps to help develop a career in management, in whatever direction they choose.

1

PLAN A PATH

Create a vision of the future: in 10 years' time, what would the ideal job involve? What are the requirements of the ideal job, such as training or gaining experience in a different field? Set goals—what will need to have been achieved and by when? Create a picture of what success will look like at each stage.

7 STAY AHEAD

Even at the top of a career, it is important to continue learning. Mentoring junior staff keeps managers abreast of new ideas.

6 BE SURE THE VISION IS STILL ATTRACTIVE

Personal situations alter and fresh avenues open up. With experience, goals can change. Question whether the vision needs to be adapted or a new course steered.

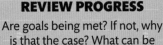

5 REVIEW PROGRESS

Are goals being met? If not, why is that the case? What can be learned from success and failure? Are the goals still appropriate, or has something changed?

3 DEAL WITH SETBACKS

Reassess values and goals. Do they still fit? Are they realistic? Are there other ways to achieve an ambition—a sideways move, perhaps? Understand that everyone has setbacks. Regain motivation and look for new opportunities.

2 BUILD A PORTABLE SKILLS BASE

Success is built on more than knowledge and technical ability. Effective communication and the ability to work with others are vital skills in any role. Anticipate what the ideal role requires, and work to develop those abilities in readiness.

Effective Networking

Networking involves establishing and maintaining a range of contacts, both inside and outside the workplace. For a manager, collaborating with a network can greatly enhance both their business and their career.

Building relationships

Every manager has a unique combination of personal skills, knowledge, and experience. By building relationships with a variety of people, managers can share their own strengths, learn from those of others, and benefit from a larger pool of expertise. Networking also provides access to influential people and can generate career opportunities.

The three stages to networking involve deciding which people to approach as contacts, finding opportunities to reach them, and maintaining those relationships. Useful contacts include decision-makers, people with interesting ideas, and those who can provide introductions to other key figures. To network successfully, a generous, responsive, and supportive attitude toward other people is essential.

Although social media tools for work-based networking (such as LinkedIn) are an excellent way to make new contacts, it is also important to meet people face to face. Informal meetings, industry events, and social meetups organized by professional associations can be useful opportunities for networking.

Six degrees of separation

Research carried out by the US psychologist Stanley Milgram in the 1960s suggests that most people can be connected to almost anyone else in the world through a chain of just six linked acquaintances. A wider scope of networking therefore offers potential access to a huge range of contacts from different industries, locations, and backgrounds. It can also help managers build their reputation and open new career opportunities.

1. LORI

As a college lecturer, **Lori** has a wide range of contacts in a variety of disciplines and professions. She sits on the board of a small conservation charity in Mexico.

SOMA

Before
The personnel manager of a small advertising agency, **Soma** wants to progress to a more globally focused company. She begins to widen her network of contacts and links up with **Lori**, a former college friend.

After
During a meetup with **Lori**, who has seen a tweet from **Juan**, **Soma** hears about the management position at **Niko**'s company. She successfully applies for the position.

5. MATT

Media manager for a brand of power tools, **Matt** takes a six-week course—also attended by **Ingrid**—in his spare time.

2. JUAN

Marine biologist **Juan** combines conservation work with professional consultancy for a number of scientific research agencies.

150 is the number of people with whom we can maintain a meaningful relationship

Robin Dunbar, *Grooming, Gossip, and the Evolution of Language*, 1996

USING A NETWORK

A network is a group of relationships that can be continually maintained in the course of daily life. The quality of a manager's contacts is more important than the quantity—having too many people with whom to maintain a relationship will make it impossible to have meaningful interactions. Contacts tend to be either transactional or collaborative in nature: transactional relationships can bring faster short-term gains, but collaborative relationships are usually more productive in the long term.

Transactional relationship

Each party views the interaction as an opportunity for personal gain.

❯ **The results** of the interaction are the most important focus in a transactional relationship.

❯ **If there is conflict**, each party is most concerned about getting the best outcome for themselves.

Collaborative relationship

Communication between parties is deeper, and the focus is on help and mutual support.

❯ **Each person considers** the other's feelings about the results of an interaction.

❯ **Resolving conflict** to everyone's satisfaction is more important than winning the conflict.

4. INGRID

A manager at a pension fund, **Ingrid** helps with the accounts of a community organization that donates to one of **Aamir**'s projects.

6. NIKO

Matt's cousin **Niko** is an artist at a multinational PR firm. She shares a post from her company advertising a management vacancy with her social network. It is seen by **Matt** and passed on via the other four linked acquaintances by social media and word of mouth.

3. AAMIR

A former colleague of **Juan's**, **Aamir** now manages donor relations for an international NGO that funds projects in the developing world.

Work/life Balance

Being a manager can be demanding, but it is important not to let it take up too much of your personal time. A good work/life balance is essential, both for mental health and for personal relationships.

Why it matters

Working overly long hours and allowing work to encroach on weekends and even vacations is a 21st-century malady. Technology and the global nature of many enterprises has introduced a 24-hour working culture that makes it difficult to switch off. It is all too tempting to fit in extra tasks at the end of a day or respond to work calls from another time zone.

Strategies such as working from home (an option exercised by 16 percent of managers in the US) can help people balance work with personal responsibilities. However, it is still important to establish boundaries between work and home life and ensure that there is enough time available for activities that relax and distract, such as going to the movies and exercising. Leisure time is for enjoying life,

Work and home life

Like most people, managers have to juggle competing demands on their time and therefore have to figure out their priorities. For some, this means completely separating work and family life; for others, it means integrating the two. The most important thing is to create a balance that works for you. The following are eight rules that can help.

WORK

Focusing exclusively on work during office hours ensures that tasks are finished on time.

> **Create time to concentrate**. Limit interruptions, such as checking email, to certain times of the day.

> **Avoid social media distractions**. Ignore all the personal online interests until you have finished work.

> **Make a list of concerns**. Do this at the end of the day so you can switch off from work when you get home.

> **Tidy your desk**. Do this as a ritual before you leave work. This will make it easier to resume work in the morning.

while exercise boosts physical and mental health. Enjoying time with friends and family is also crucial because they provide a vital support network.

Vacations—ideally more than a week long—are excellent for recharging the batteries, especially if the "out of office" message is in place and colleagues know to make contact only in an emergency. As more companies now recognize, the work/life balance matters every day—because overworking can damage mental health as well as office and personal relationships.

82%
of managers think that flexible working is beneficial to their business

Flexible Working, The Institute of Leadership and Management

BALANCING WORK AND FAMILY LIFE

Forbes magazine suggests that working parents should give up five things to lessen the load: their pride about asking for help when they need it; the belief that time must always be split evenly (work or home may at times need more attention); the idea that they should neglect their own interests ("me" time matters); the desire to keep children endlessly happy; and guilt (working couples can still be great parents).

HOME

Relationships and leisure are vital aspects of life and should not be crowded out by work.

> **Don't seek perfection.** Try to allot a fixed time span for necessary work to allow space for leisure activities.

> **Maximize personal time.** Where possible, get outside help with chores you may dislike, such as housework.

> **Share jobs at home.** Involve the children, who benefit from feeling responsible.

> **Create downtime.** This is for taking a break even from scheduled leisure activities.

Coping with Stress

Stress affects mental and physical health, as well as the ability to perform well at work. Managers who learn how to respond to pressure can maintain their well-being and that of their team.

Recognizing and addressing stress

Stress is the adverse response to excessive pressures—a feeling of being unable to cope and that everything is out of control. Although everyone may have these feelings for short periods when experienced over the long term, the effects of stress can be serious. Various hormones released in the body to boost energy in an emergency, such as adrenalin, may help an individual meet a tight deadline, but remaining on high alert over long periods can lead to anxiety, insomnia, and a weakened immune system, among other ill effects.

As a manager, it is important to recognize signs of stress in yourself and address them, since it will also impact your team if stress is expressed in behaviors such as loss of focus or uncharacteristic bursts of anger.

There are several life events that can trigger high stress levels (see below). Regarding work-related stressors, employers in many countries have a legal responsibility for providing a safe place to work, including managing work-related stress. Aside from raising issues with superiors, individuals can use many strategies to build resilience (see right).

Weathering the storm

A variety of domestic and work problems can trigger unhealthy levels of stress. Many people try to carry on regardless, believing that "giving in" is a sign of weakness. This only worsens the situation. Health experts strongly recommend taking control of the situation, building emotional strength, maintaining a strong social network, and staying positive.

FAMILY COMMITMENTS

Stay connected to the team by chatting with them and managing by walking around.

Keep things in perspective—most "crises" don't deserve catastrophe status.

THE STRESS SCALE

As a manager, it is important to be aware of how life events can affect your stress levels. Researchers Richard Raye and Thomas Holmes devised a scale for measuring stress by allocating a certain number of points to each event. If a person exceeds 150 points on the scale, they are likely to become ill. Some top-rated events include:

Event	Points
Death of a spouse/partner	100
Divorce	73
Marital separation	65
Death of a close family member	63
Illness or injury	53

"The great thing, then... is to make our nervous system our ally instead of our enemy."

William James, philosopher and psychologist, 1890

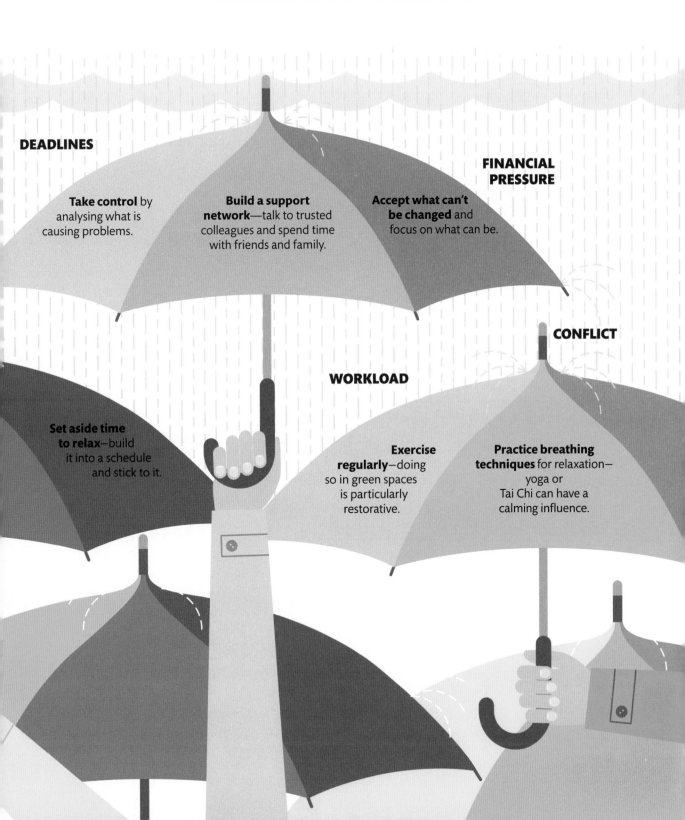

DEADLINES

Take control by analysing what is causing problems.

Build a support network—talk to trusted colleagues and spend time with friends and family.

FINANCIAL PRESSURE

Accept what can't be changed and focus on what can be.

CONFLICT

WORKLOAD

Set aside time to relax—build it into a schedule and stick to it.

Exercise regularly—doing so in green spaces is particularly restorative.

Practice breathing techniques for relaxation—yoga or Tai Chi can have a calming influence.

Learning and Development

Taking responsibility for learning can not only support career development but also lead to greater personal fulfillment. Opportunities for growth are not limited only to years in formal education—they can be a lifelong pursuit.

Constant growth

Learning is the acquisition of knowledge and skills, whereas development is the gradual mastery of those skills, putting knowledge into practice and incorporating it into everyday work. Both are important for growth in a managerial career.

Part of success in this area involves having the right mindset. In her 2006 book *Mindset*, psychologist Professor Carol Dweck talks about "the growth mindset." This allows people to believe that they are not limited by circumstances but can improve and seize opportunities to learn and grow.

The other factor is actively putting processes in place. Managers may be offered ongoing training, but they can still take charge of their own development—for instance, by prompting feedback from line managers to help identify blind spots. They might also do a personal audit, rating their skills in key parts of the role and pinpointing areas to improve. These findings can then become part of a development plan they can follow (see below). The plan might focus on areas such as skills, growth, and relationships, but it should be aligned with the manager's organizational role, and changes should have the support of line managers.

Reevaluation
As circumstances change and new opportunities arise, it is vital to go back to the plan and check that it still works.

"You don't learn to walk by following rules. You learn by doing and falling over."
Richard Branson, 2014

Onward and upward

A development plan to advance your career consists of a set of questions and answers, combined with a schedule for achieving your goals. It should begin with a vision of the future: What will it look and feel like? What learning is needed to achieve it? Steps that appear too large can be daunting, so the plan should be broken down into smaller milestones. It should also be a mixture of formal and informal learning.

Over 80% of senior professionals believe that executive education/leadership development has improved their skills

VanDyck Silveira, CEO of FT | IE Corporate Learning Alliance, 2017

Informal learning
This is an ongoing process of keeping an eye on how things work—and watching other people.

Taking a leap
Trying out new learning methods, developing new skills, and being curious all contribute to developing an enterprising mindset.

Formal learning
This is structured, classroom-based or online learning. It is usually delivered by an institution and leads to a qualification.

INFORMAL LEARNING

Learning informally on the job, particularly on challenging projects, is where managers will gain the most experience.

❯ **Failure provides** a rich learning experience, helping you to reflect on how things could be handled better.

❯ **Taking risks** moves you out of your comfort zone. Accepting a challenge and doing something new adds to your experience and helps to expand your knowledge and skills.

❯ **Seeking feedback** and accepting it shows how your actions appear to others and how they can be improved.

Learning Styles

Staff training should never be a case of "one size fits all". The manager who understands how both they and their staff learn best will be well equipped to choose the most effective types of training.

Routes to learning goals

Since the 1970s, researchers have explored the different ways in which people like to learn. Their work can help managers to identify the optimum learning style of individual employees, and match it to an appropriate training course.

Three well-known expositions of learning styles are Walter Barbe's VAK model from 1979, which explores how people absorb knowledge; the Felder-Silverman model from 1988, which links learning style to personality type; and the Dunn and Dunn model from 1978, which focuses on influences that can affect how an individual learns (see box, far right). Other styles include the Honey and Mumford model, which links theorist David Kolb's idea of a four-stage learning cycle with four types of personality, each of which is best suited to one of the four learning stages (see right).

A range of questionnaires based on such models can help employees discover their own preferred style. Finding training to match styles is increasingly viable as technology can deliver courses in many formats. All learning styles are equal, but at times it may be helpful for people leave their comfort zone to learn in new ways.

> ## "Learning is the process whereby knowledge is created through the transformation of experience."
>
> David A. Kolb, American educational theorist, 1971

EXPERIENCING

ACTIVISTS
Like to try things out and become immersed in new experiences. They may rush, however, and take unnecessary risks.

APPLYING AND TESTING

PRAGMATISTS
Like to apply their learning to the real world. They are less keen on theory, preferring to get on with things and try them out.

TRYING THINGS OUT

The learning cycle

In 1984 theorist David Kolb proposed the idea of a four-stage learning cycle, shown here on the outer rim of the wheel of learning (right). The first stage is experiencing something, followed by thinking or reflecting on it, then forming ideas about it, and finally, trying it out. In 1986 Peter Honey and Alan Mumford added to the idea, identifying four personalities that perform best at a given stage in the cycle. An activist likes the hands-on experience, a reflector enjoys thinking things through, a theorist forms ideas, and a pragmatist is someone who applies the knowledge.

HANDS-ON EXPERIENCE

REVIEWING

REFLECTORS

Watch, gather information, and reflect on what has happened. They tend to be careful and thorough, taking time to think before acting.

LEARNING CYCLE

An effective learning cycle, as explained by David Kolb, has four stages, as seen here on the wheel's outer rim. Peter Honey and Alan Mumford suggest that each stage best suits one of four different types of personality.

OBSERVATION AND REFLECTION

THEORISTS

Like to work with facts and defined concepts, to question and analyze information, and to create logical models. They are less suited to unstructured working environments.

...IZATION AND ABSTRACTION

DRAWING CONCLUSIONS

THE VAK MODEL

Walter Barbe in the US described three learning styles in his VAK model. Most people prefer one of them but often use all three.

> **Visual:** by seeing or writing down information
> **Auditory:** by listening
> **Kinesthetic:** by actively doing things

FELDER-SILVERMAN MODEL

Engineering professor Richard Felder and psychologist Linda Silverman extended the VAK model by linking learning styles to personality types.

> **Sensing:** prefer concrete thinking and facts
> **Intuitive:** prefer concepts and ideas
> **Verbal:** like written and spoken information
> **Visual:** prefer diagrams, images, and charts
> **Active:** prefer to try things out
> **Reflective:** like to think things through, often alone
> **Sequential:** like an orderly approach in small steps
> **Global:** like large steps and holistic thinking

LEARNING ENVIRONMENTS

In the 1970s, American professors Rita Dunn and Kenneth Dunn reviewed 80 years of research into how children learn. They found five preferences that could help identify an individual's optimal learning environment—something that applies equally to adults.

> **Environmental:** how do noise, light, and temperature affect the learner?
> **Emotional:** does the learner need structure, guidance, and motivational support?
> **Sociological:** does the learner like to work alone or in a team?
> **Physiological:** at what time of day does the learner learn best?
> **Psychological:** do they handle information analytically, reflectively, or impulsively?

Staying Alert

Managers should be optimistic when starting a new business or project, but a certain degree of caution, and remaining alert to possible pitfalls, will make success more likely.

Striking a balance

For a new venture to thrive, a manager must have faith in their staff, systems, processes, and technology. Blind trust, however, can prove hazardous. For example, a manager might believe so much in a particular person or idea that danger signals are missed. So a balance must be struck between accepting that everything will work according to plan and constant double-checking, which is extremely time-consuming and demotivates employees, who will feel that they are not trusted. In competitive organizations, distrust and suspicion are not unusual, but in a heightened form they become paranoia. If such feelings persist, they can be both personally and

Watching the future

Andy Grove, the founder of Intel, set out his thoughts on success in his bestselling book *Only the Paranoid Survive* (1996). He warned that success breeds complacency and that complacency leads to failure—that a certain amount of fear can be a useful tool in certain business contexts. He believed that the best managers are those who are always watching for the next threat and that this involves a certain kind of paranoia. He coined the term "strategic inflection point" to describe the point at which change becomes inevitable— and said that depending on how they meet it, companies either thrive or fail.

STRATEGIC INFLECTION POINT

GROWTH PHASE

2. Turning point

However successful the venture, managers must stay alert to any changes in the operating environment; the sooner any threats are spotted, the sooner they can be acted on. These inflection points require changes to the way business is conducted.

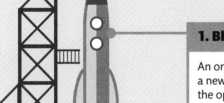

1. Blast off

An organization launches a new product or service. If the operating environment is favorable, the venture may be a success from the outset.

professionally ruinous, and lead to the erosion of the vital relationship between management and staff.

The best approach is not to assume that things will go wrong, but to stay alert for warning signs and plan for possible future problems. Crucially, this requires being mindful to external threats – especially those posed by rival organizations in the operational environment (see below).

FURTHER GROWTH

DECLINE

3a. Success

New ideas may guide the venture into a period of further growth. However, managers should not be complacent; there will be more inflection points in the future.

> **"By failing to prepare, you are preparing to fail."**
>
> Benjamin Franklin, one of the
> Founding Fathers of the United States

CASE STUDY

Intel's change of direction

When it was founded in 1968, American technology corporation Intel produced memory chips for computers. However, during the 1970s, under the leadership of Andy Grove, it faced a strategic inflection point: Japanese companies were dominating the memory market. Intel changed direction and began producing microprocessors instead—a decision that saved it from failure and reset its course for success.

3b. Failure

If the organization fails to change, its venture will not succeed. It will not be able to compete with rival organizations that have adapted to the new environment.

Accountability

Managers have to be accountable, which means being answerable for what they do, taking ownership of a sphere of activity, and accepting the consequences of what happens. This is essential for good performance.

Taking the strain

Accountability and responsibility are sometimes confused, but there are subtle differences between the two. For example, the last person in the office may be responsible for locking the doors at night so that the office is secure.

However, if the office is broken into and the equipment is stolen, accountability will lie with the manager. It is the manager who will have to investigate what happened, explain the situation to their superiors, and ensure that it never happens again.

A manager, therefore, is answerable not only for their own actions but also for those of the people they manage. However, this does not mean that the manager should be a scapegoat for anything that goes wrong. If, for example, a deadline

Team accountability

A manager has to be accountable for their actions, decisions, and the overall fate of their enterprise. However, to achieve success, they must also instill accountability in their employees. Just as a manager is answerable to their superiors for the actions of their team, so the individuals in a team should be accountable to their manager. This means that everyone owns their share of the enterprise and feels responsible for the outcome.

Taking charge
A manager should have an overview of everything that is happening and ensure that each person accepts their responsibilities. Crucially, the manager accepts that they are accountable for the team.

Conducting the team
Just doing a job is not enough. Supporting others and not allocating blame are important for good teamwork.

is missed, the manager should be accountable but should also investigate who may have erred and speak to those individuals accordingly. For this reason, staff should also be encouraged to take ownership of their part of the process. Accountable staff boost performance and help maintain a positive and ethical culture. Without accountability, people tend to blame each other, and nothing is resolved or improved.

LEARNING TO BE ACCOUNTABLE

Being accountable requires courage as it often means:

> **Having difficult conversations** with people about performance

> **Ensuring that each person** understands their responsibilities

> **Taking hard decisions** for the greater good of the team

> **Exercising judgment** in the face of conflicting evidence

> **Being honest and open** with others about what is happening

> **Sacrificing your own interests** for the sake of what is right

> **Holding up a mirror** to your own conduct

Accepting responsibility

Each team member has a part to play, ensuring that they carry out their responsibilities to the best of their ability.

"**The** benefits and possibilities **that are** created by being personally accountable **are** countless."

Jay Fiset, *Reframe Your Blame: How to Be Personally Accountable*, 2006

CREATE THE RIGHT CULTURE

Encouraging accountability in your team means primarily accepting it yourself—following through on your commitments and recognizing that others are dependent on what you do. It also means keeping team members involved in your decisions so that they are fully aware of their own responsibilities. By setting an example of accountability, you can inspire people in your team to follow suit.

Developing New Routines

The best managers not only keep an eye on their teams, but also analyse their own behavior and recognize the effect that it has on others.

Self-analysis

In a busy and often stressful workplace, it is essential for a manager to take time to reflect on how their behavior affects others. Far from being a sign of insecurity, self-analysis is an important part of self-development, and without it a manager is unlikely to succeed.

Management involves exercising judgment in situations in which not all the facts are known. In order to exercise good judgment, a manager must therefore understand their own values and beliefs and recognize how their own biases affect the way they view particular situations. They also need to understand that others might perceive things differently. Finally, they must know what has to be achieved and what a good outcome will look like. Taking all of this into account, they have to decide what the most effective course of action is likely to be.

Routine behavior

Self-understanding is a good start, but adopting new habits as a result is essential if change is to occur. A habit is a routine of behavior, conscious or subconscious, that is repeated regularly. People often think about habits as being purely physical, like taking a walk every morning, but everyone has habits of thinking, too. Reflecting on what these are and embedding new, positive patterns of thinking is vital for success.

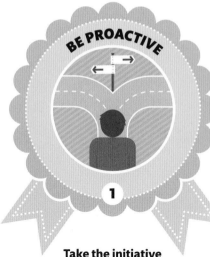

Take the initiative
Proactive managers take responsibility for issues over which they know they have control and use their own initiative to solve problems.

Seven habits

In 1989, American businessman Stephen Covey wrote the bestselling book *The 7 Habits of Highly Effective People*, which inspired millions of people to make better decisions and build better relationships. Covey identified seven habits that people should cultivate to improve their lives. The first three habits focus on moving from dependence to independence; the second three concern cooperation; and the final habit concerns continuous growth and renewal. Although intended for the general public, the habits are easy to adapt to a management setting.

Respect others
The best managers think "win-win." This means that they understand the viewpoint of others and solve problems in a way that is best for everyone, not just for themselves.

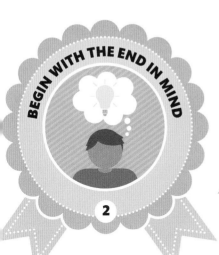

BEGIN WITH THE END IN MIND

2

Look to the future
Successful managers know what they want to achieve and have an end goal in mind. This helps them understand the steps that are needed to reach their destination.

PUT FIRST THINGS FIRST

3

Prioritize
When prioritizing tasks, effective managers consider not only which task is most urgent but also which is the most important.

"Be a light, not a judge. Be a model, not a critic. Be part of the solution, not the problem."

Stephen Covey, *The 7 Habits of Highly Effective People*, 1989

SEEK FIRST TO UNDERSTAND THEN TO BE UNDERSTOOD

5

Understand the problem
Before rushing in with a solution, emotionally intelligent managers listen to problems and try to see them through the eyes of others.

SYNERGIZE

6

Consider other views
Appreciating different viewpoints enables constructive managers to build on their strengths, mitigate their weaknesses, and enrich their original ideas.

SHARPEN THE SAW

7

Keep growing
Effective managers stay sharp, maintaining a habit of self-renewal and growth in order to remain productive.

Index

Acknowledgments

Dorling Kindersley would like to thank Matthew Williams for additional writing; Alethea Doran and Jemima Dunne for editing; Janashree Singha, Steve Stetford, and Debra Wolter for proofreading; and Vanessa Bird for indexing.

Credits

p.30_31 IT management '*How much data do we create every day?*' Marr. B;. Forbes, 2018; **p.100 Consequence model** *The Decison Book*, Krogus & Tschäppeler, 2008 (b). **pp.122–123 MBO model** *The Practice of Management*, Drucker, P., 1954; **BSC theory** "The Balanced Scorecard," Kaplan and Norton, 1992. **p.146 FSNP model** "Developmental Sequence in Small Groups," Bruce Tuckman, *Psychological Bulletin*, 1965. **p.196 The Johari Window** *The Johari Window*, Luft and Ingram, 1995. **pp.208–209 VAK model** *Teaching through Modality Strengths: Concepts Practices*, Walter, B., 1979; **Felder-Silverman model** *Learning and Teaching Styles in Engineering Education*, Felder and Silverman, 1988; **Dunn and Dunn model** *Teaching Students through Their Individual Learning Styles*, Dunn, R. and Dunn, K., 1978; **Four-stage learning** *Experiential Learning: Experience as the Source of Learning and Development*, Kolb, D. A., 1984. **p.210–211 Strategic inflection point graph** *Only the Paranoid Survive*, Grove, A., 1996.